How to Discover Your Vocation

Marriage, Priesthood, Consecrated Life, Permanent
Diaconate, Single Life

by
Fr. Stephen Wang

*All booklets are published thanks to the
generous support of the members of the
Catholic Truth Society*

 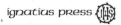

2

Contents

How to use this booklet

This booklet is written for Catholics who are trying to discover what direction their life is going in and what plans God has for them. It will help you to think and pray about your vocation and begin to understand where God is leading you in your life. Don't feel you have to read the whole booklet through from start to finish. You can look at the table of contents and dip into whichever sections seem relevant to your life.

At the beginning of each chapter there is a prayer or meditation. You could use these in your own prayer time. At the end of each chapter one or two people explain something about how they discovered their own vocation. These testimonies are included to show the many different ways that God is at work in our lives. Take a look at them even if you are not reading that particular chapter.

It's important to seek God's will and to be open to his plans. But there is a danger of becoming so anxious about your vocation, so caught up in a future that does not yet exist, that you forget about living the life God has already given you. So yes, do put some time and effort into considering your vocation – be open, be generous, be brave. It is a wonderful adventure! But at the same time be grateful for the person you are now, and for the work God has given you to do today.

Acknowledgements

I am very grateful to the following people who have read all or parts of this text and made invaluable suggestions about how it could be improved: Andrew Gallagher, Joanna Gilbert, Andrzej Jaxa-Chamiec, Fr Luke Jolly OSB, Sr Cathy Jones RA, Brian O'Mahony, Rev James Richards, Hannah Vaughan-Spruce, Elizabeth Wang, Mary Wang, and Clare Watkins. Various friends wrote the story of their vocation for me. I have given them some anonymity by just using their first names. I am enormously grateful to them for their honest and thoughtful responses.

The quotation from Joanna Gilbert at the end of chapter 7 is from chapter 1 of *Touched by God*, Ed. Laurentia Johns (London: Burns & Oates, 2008), pp. 4 and 27. The other quotations are, as far as I know, in the public domain, or given to me by friends.

Fr Stephen Wang

I. VOCATION AND DISCERNMENT

1. Do I have a vocation?

"God calls all the souls he has created to love him with their whole being, here and thereafter, which means that he calls all of them to holiness, to perfection, to a close following of him and obedience to his will. But he does not ask all souls to show their love by the same works, to climb to heaven by the same ladder, to achieve goodness in the same way. What sort of work, then, must I do? Which is *my* road to heaven? In what kind of life am I *to sanctify myself?*" (*Blessed Charles de Foucauld*)

Created to share God's love – The fundamental vocation of every human being is to love. This is not obvious to everyone today. Many people believe that human life is just an accident, a chance product of evolution, a meaningless event in a vast mechanical universe. It is certainly true that our lives have been shaped by many different forces, but there is a much deeper truth that we can discover through faith: *Every single human being has been created by God out of love*. He made us so that we could know his love, and share that love with others, and delight in that love forever in the glory of heaven. So whatever you feel about your own worth – *never doubt that your life has a meaning*. God loves you and cares for you. You are precious to him and he has a purpose for your life, even if that does not seem very clear to you.

What is a vocation? – The word 'vocation' comes from the Latin word that means 'calling'. For the Christian a vocation is not just something that God calls us to do, it is also the person God calls us to be. When Jesus called his first disciples by the Lake of Galilee it wasn't just so that they could help him in his work, it was so that their lives could be transformed through his friendship and love. We have been called to follow Christ, the Son of God, the eternal Word of the Father, who came to save us and to lead us back to heaven with him. He has sent his Holy Spirit so that we can share in his divine life even now, and express that life by trying to love him and to love our neighbour. The Christian vocation is a call to share in the life of the Most Holy Trinity.

Vocation as a call to holiness – One way of expressing this is to say that the fundamental human vocation is the call to holiness, the call to be a saint. The saints are not just heroic people who live in history books; they are ordinary Christians who have tried to live their faith without holding anything back – to love God with their whole hearts, to love those around them without counting the cost, to work at what is worthwhile with dedication and purpose, to be people of joy and kindness and prayerfulness. *All of us are called to be saints* – however weak or sinful we feel. This is not so much a command as a promise that God makes:

he promises us, by giving us his Holy Spirit, that he will help us to find our true happiness in following him, and that he will give us whatever we need for the journey.

You already have a vocation – This vocation to holiness is already a part of your life, given to you at your baptism, and it is so important to remember that. Whatever situation you are in now, however unsatisfactory it seems, you already have a vocation. You might be working, studying, travelling, unemployed, or caring for someone at home; you might be very content, or utterly miserable; full of hope, or close to despair. Whatever your situation, you can trust that God is with you, and that he calls you to be holy in this very situation. Things may well change – and perhaps they need to; but at this moment you must have the confidence to believe that *even now there is a meaning and a purpose to your life;* and that you can begin to fulfil that by everyday acts of love and kindness and patience.

Living well in the present – This call to live well in the present is the *Little Way* recommended by St Thérèse of Lisieux – the importance of simply doing your duty, saying your prayers, loving your neighbour, bearing your sufferings; and doing all this with a generous and loving heart. It is not very dramatic, but it is the secret of holiness, and it reminds us that *your first and fundamental vocation is not something to be discovered in the future – it is living the Christian life in the here and now.* Perhaps this is all God wants of you for the moment. You must avoid the temptation of thinking that your Christian life can only properly begin in the future, when everything is crystal clear. And if you do not discover a more concrete vocation, or if you are to die young, then you should not feel that you have wasted your life, or that your life is unfinished or unfulfilled.

Vocation as a call to a concrete 'state of life' – Christ has always called some people to follow him in concrete ways, by giving them a more specific vocation. In previous generations, the word 'vocation' would only have been used to describe the lives of priests and religious – because these people had in some sense been called 'away' from an ordinary life to a life of celibacy and service in the Church. But today the word 'vocation' is rightly used also of marriage, permanent diaconate, consecrated life, and some forms of single life – because each of these is a wholehearted commitment that we make in response to an invitation from the Lord. These concrete vocations are also known as 'states of life', because we make a lifelong commitment to living our Christian faith in a particular context. *This lifelong commitment becomes the place in which we live out our fundamental vocation to holiness.* God calls us all to be saints; and sometimes he calls us to be saints in a particular way – as husbands or wives, as priests or deacons or consecrated persons.

Vocation as a call to be the unique person you are made to be – There is yet another level to 'vocation'. Each saint is unique, and you are called to be holy not just in a general way, but in the particular way that God has made you to be. *God created you as a unique individual, and calls you by a name that no-one else has been given. You reflect Christ's love and show something of his face in a way that no-one else can.* This is *your 'personal' vocation – the call to be the person you are meant to be.* The more you discover who you are, and the more you discover what lies deepest in your heart, the more you will be able to discern what God's will is for you and what direction he wants you to take in life. Your lifelong vocational commitments and the particular path of holiness that you are called to follow will inevitably grow out of the person God created you to be.

Sally, member of a Focolare community:

"Discovering my vocation was part of a life changing experience. I am from Northern Ireland and growing up in Belfast I was no stranger to the harsher side of life. Having seen injustice and cruelty on all sides in that senseless conflict, at the age of 17, I decided that not only politicians but even God had forsaken Belfast. What changed everything for me was when, through my contact with the Focolare Movement, I saw Christians who were united. They not only spoke about the revolutionary power of the Gospel to change people and situations but they made it the foundation of their everyday life. That in turn gave me the strength to change my life and to begin to make a difference to the situation around me. I realised that when I was with them I was at home. I felt a deep peace. I was completely free. When I was with them, I was the best of myself. I knew then I wanted to live like this 24/7. It is a choice I have never regretted."

Fr Digby, Diocesan priest:

"Somehow I just knew what I had to do to be true to myself. And the strong pull within me was to apply for the priesthood. I can resonate strongly with both why the word 'vocation' is used in this way and also with how those in the scriptures who were called by God also had a certain fear about saying yes – the 'hound of heaven' experience perhaps. Looking back to my teens when this experience was first felt, I feel blessed that there was this clarity - it's never left me in 45 years. The challenge has been to live it out in a way that is alive and authentic, starting afresh every day. Sometimes I say to people who are considering major life decisions "I made the 'mistake' of continuing to pray – that way I kept hearing the call!" If I hadn't kept up the prayer maybe I would have blocked out what the Lord really wanted, but I can't see how I'd have been happy. There is a phrase you hear: 'In Your will is our peace'."

2. What are the different Christian vocations?

"Love makes us seek what is good; love makes us better persons. It is love that prompts men and women to marry and form a family, to have children. It is love that prompts others to embrace the religious life or become priests. Love makes you reach out to others in need, whoever they are, wherever they are. Every genuine human love is a reflection of the Love that is God himself." (*Pope John Paul II*)

A variety of gifts and callings – Every person is different. We have different natural gifts; and we have different spiritual gifts. And for his own mysterious reasons, God calls some people to one way of life, and some to another; sometimes by planting a deep desire in their hearts, or sometimes by pulling them in a new and unexpected direction. Here are the different 'states of life' that God can call us to.

Marriage – *Through marriage a husband and wife give themselves to each other without reservation*, promising to love each other faithfully for the rest of their lives, sharing their joys and sufferings in whatever circumstances life brings them. They express their love through their sexual union, which brings them together in the closest intimacy and opens them to the gift of new life. They build not just a relationship but a home and a family and a place of welcome for others too. You do not need to be a Christian, of course, to get married; but for Christians the natural union of marriage is transformed into a sacrament. For a Christian couple *the call to love each other in this way becomes at the same time an invitation to follow Christ and to give their lives wholeheartedly to him in love and service.* The love shown between a Christian husband and wife becomes a sign of the radical love shown by Christ in his life, death and resurrection. Christian marriage is not just an expression of human affection, it is a sacrament of the love of Christ, a way for husband and wife to minister to each other and to their children. And in this way the Christian family becomes a place where others can see the beauty and power of Christ's redeeming love, a love that is often obscured in our fallen world. This is why marriage is a Christian vocation.

Consecrated life – Catholics often use the term 'religious' to describe those who have taken vows of poverty, chastity (or more precisely: lifelong celibacy) and obedience. The most helpful phrase to use is 'consecrated life'. This is the way of life embraced by all those who dedicate themselves to the Lord by making these lifelong vows when they are recognised and accepted by the Church. These vows are sometimes called the 'evangelical counsels'. Every Christian, of course, is dedicated to the Lord, and has promised through baptism to give his or her life to him. Every Christian longs to live a life of holiness.

What is a Sacrament?

But those who consecrate themselves in this way are responding to a call *to live as Christ lived, and to model their lives more directly on his own way of life – poor, chaste, and obedient – making their hearts more free for prayer and service.* They show us more clearly something about the concrete reality of Christ's love. They also give us a glimpse of the purity of the love we all hope to share in heaven, when our lives will be uncluttered by possessions or family responsibilities, and our hearts will be solely centred on God. The consecrated life includes monks and nuns in enclosed communities, religious brothers and sisters in active communities, and also many others who live alone or who live and work 'in the world' who have taken the three vows.

The single life – There are also many people who have made a personal commitment to the single life even though they have not taken formal vows. The commitment might have been a personal choice, to give them the freedom to serve the Lord in a particular way or follow a particular path; or it might have been a process of willingly coming to accept the single way of life, through force of circumstances or other decisions. These people, as long as that commitment remains, are equally called to show the love of Christ through their lives, and to *put their freedom at the service of others in their work and prayer.* In this sense the committed single life is rightly considered a vocation.

Priesthood – All Christians are called to live a 'priestly' life, which means they offer their whole lives in prayer and service to God in union with the offering of Jesus the High Priest. This is our 'baptismal' priesthood. The 'ministerial' priest, however, through the sacrament of ordination, shares in the priesthood of Christ in a special way. His very being is transfigured in this sacrament, so that *he can represent Christ the Good Shepherd for us, Christ as the Head of the Church.* He not only offers his own life to the Father in sacrifice, as all Christians do, but he also stands before the Church and ministers to us as Christ 'in person'. When he teaches with the authority of the Church then Christ teaches; when he forgives sins in the sacrament of Penance then Christ forgives; when he offers the Sacrifice of the Mass then Christ offers that Sacrifice; when he loves and supports and cares for his people then Christ is present with his people. Because of the wishes of Jesus himself, confirmed by the tradition of the Church throughout the centuries, the ministerial priesthood is reserved for men (see chapter 10 for further thoughts about women and the priesthood). In the Western Church the priesthood is also reserved, ordinarily, for single men who are willing to make a lifelong commitment to celibacy, for in this way they can give their whole hearts and minds to the service of the Lord and to the love of his people.

The permanent diaconate – The diaconate is also a sacrament of ordination. The permanent deacon, who may be single or married, dedicates his life to serving others. His ministry of service focuses on three areas: assisting at the altar in the celebration of the sacraments; preaching the Word of God and leading people in prayer; and reaching out in loving service to the practical and spiritual needs of others, especially of the poor and those outside the normal confines of the Church. Traditionally the permanent deacon works closely with his diocesan bishop. Most permanent deacons, in practice, serve the greater part of their time within their home parish. But there are many who work as chaplains in schools, prisons, hospitals, etc. Others are in full-time employment where their work is itself 'diaconal': teachers, social workers, nurses, doctors, etc. *Their ordination brings a specific grace that allows their life of service to be consecrated in a special way.*

Each vocation is a call to follow Christ – The lifestyle and demands of each particular vocation are very different, but there are some common threads. *Each vocation is a commitment to love in a certain way* and to draw closer to others – whether that closeness is through marriage or service or prayer. Each vocation challenges us to live our faith more deeply and to follow Christ more closely. Each vocation, if it is lived generously, will involve times of deep happiness and joy. Each vocation, if it is lived faithfully, will almost inevitably involve moments of great suffering and sacrifice. We should not think that one vocation is easier than another. Genuine love always costs a great deal, and brings great rewards. In one sense, to make a commitment to lifelong celibacy as a priest or consecrated person seems like a more radical choice, because it pulls us away from the natural joys of family life. But to live an authentic Christian marriage today, and to uphold Christian values in family life, requires enormous courage and commitment – it 'costs' as much, if not more, than celibacy. The important point is not to compare the value of different vocations, but to appreciate the value of each one, and to discover which one is right for you.

Silvia, wife and mother:
"I thought I always wanted to get married. What little girl doesn't play house and dream of growing up, getting married to a wonderful man and raising their children? But I had been thinking about being a nun too. Soon after entering university, I met a really nice guy who was also a good Catholic. We prayed together and talked about marriage, but the idea of religious life still lingered. I thought if God wanted it to happen, he'd let me know in some way or other. After three or so years, many of which were spent apart from each other, we got to know each other very well. I'm sure by then we knew what we wanted, and we were at peace that it was God's will. It all just seemed to fall into place. I know it isn't so easy for everyone. So, we were

married a little more than four years after we met. Even then, at 22 and 24, we were very young! Now, nine children later, I am so thankful for our marriage and family. God is so good."

Mike, husband and father:

"A defining point in my faith was meeting a priest at Lourdes who was very humble in his faith. I knew that I needed to start thinking seriously about putting God at the centre of my life. I had a real fear that the only way that I could serve God fully was to become a priest and I was not sure if I could do it. Then someone told me that becoming a priest was not the only way to serve God. I knew this already, but having someone else say it opened me up to other possibilities. As so often happens with God, it was at the time I was finally becoming comfortable with and practising my Catholic faith that I met my future wife Sophie. We started our relationship with our faith in common and this was a great foundation to start from. There have been no "Road to Emmaus" moments in my life, but I have always had a strong sense that God has been with me on my journey. Getting married was a wonderful experience, being able to make a commitment to my wife with friends, family and God present. I am not a priest, but the more I find out about my faith and the more I live out my vocation of marriage, the more I realise it is a call to serve and to make myself a gift to my wife, and now that my wife is pregnant, to make myself a gift to my expanding family."

3. What does it mean to be single?

"If you are who you are meant to be, you will set the world on fire." (*St Catherine of Siena*)

The single life – People are single for many different reasons. If you are single at this moment, whatever the reason, you can believe that your life right now has immense value. Every person is called to a life of holiness, and in this sense every person who is single is called to live out their Christian vocation, wherever it might be leading them in the future. Your work, your study, your friendships, your care for your family, your service to others – these are all areas of life in which you are meeting Christ and bringing his love to others. Give thanks to God for your life and for the opportunities presented to you.

It would not be quite right to say that every single person has a vocation to be single, in the sense of a lifelong commitment – and we must be careful of the way we talk about the single vocation. It would be best, perhaps, to say that the single life is a concrete vocation only when it has been chosen as a response to a sense of calling; or at least when it has been willingly accepted as a long-term way of life in response to circumstances. This chapter lists some of the situations that single people find themselves in, and gives one or two thoughts about how to approach them.

Just getting on with life – Many people are single and happy about that and just getting on with life. You might be doing some fulfilling and worthwhile work. You might be hard at your studies. You might be involved in some all-consuming project. You might be too young or busy or distracted or happy to be thinking big thoughts about future commitments. That's fine! Be happy and be holy. *Just make sure that now and then you stop to think about your vocation as a Christian, and to ask the Lord in prayer if he has any other plans for you.* You have every right to make the most of this situation, without undue anxiety – as long as you are open to other possibilities as well.

Those who are searching – Many single people are hoping to discover a more particular vocation and to make a lifelong commitment to marriage or priesthood or the consecrated life, but they are unsure about which one. Or they are clear about wanting to get married, but still looking for a husband or wife. Or they are dating and wondering if this is the right person. If this is the case, you can follow all the suggestions in this booklet about how to discern your vocation and how, at the right time, to come to a decision. *Remember that your happiness does not just lie in the future.* God wants you to find peace and to live a life of holiness in this present moment, even if your future is unclear. He wants you to trust him: to do everything you can, but to be patient as well.

Those who are struggling – Some people are single not through choice but through circumstances. They wish they were not single, but they cannot see any way out. Perhaps you are not drawn to marriage, or unable to find a husband or wife. Perhaps you want to be a priest or live a consecrated life, but you have been 'turned down' by the diocese or religious order. Perhaps you are caring for a sick relative or a child and you are not able to take on any other commitments. Perhaps you are sick yourself. There may be other difficulties in your life that make you feel you cannot pursue the vocation you would like to. Or perhaps you have a valid marriage, but are now separated from your husband or wife, without any apparent hope of reconciliation or of being granted an annulment; so that your day-to-day life is like that of a single person, only without the possibility of entering into a new marriage. *In all these situations it is very important to trust in God and to believe that he knows what he is doing with your life.* There may be very real suffering and disappointment involved, and you can certainly hope and pray that the situation will change. But you also need to accept that this is God's will for you in this present moment, *to carry this cross with as much humility and love as is possible.* Don't give in to despair or self-pity. Live your Catholic faith, and trust that this is happening for a reason. *Your vocation right now, without a doubt, is to show the love of Christ in these difficult circumstances.* And through that love, if it is his will, he will lead you to a new stage, or help you to find new meaning in this present situation.

Committed to the single life – Some people have in effect made a personal commitment to lifelong celibacy, even without taking any formal vows. Some choose celibacy because they wish to give their lives in service to others, or because it allows them to follow a particular path in life. Some recognise that they are unlikely to get married, for all sorts of different reasons, and they willingly accept this and commit their lives to following Christ and living their faith as single people. *Those who accept the single life in this way, for whatever reason, can rightly think of this as their vocation – a call from God to live a life of holiness in this context, which will bear great fruit and will be richly rewarded.* But perhaps we should not necessarily think of this form of celibacy as a lifelong vocation, because the circumstances might change. If you are single, and at peace about being single, but then something unexpected comes up, and you feel pulled towards another vocation – then you are perfectly free to look into that!

Consecrated single life – Some people do take lifelong vows of poverty, celibacy and obedience, but continue to live and work in the world. Their vows mean that, in the language of the Church, they are living a consecrated life. *Those who are consecrated have the assurance of God and of the Church that this is indeed a lifelong commitment and vocation.*

Odile, consecrated single person in the Nôtre Dame de Vie Secular Institute:

"In my story it seems to me that it was God who was looking out for me more than myself and my vocation came in a way as a surprise. I wanted to get married and have children (eight of them) and at the same time, I could feel that God was calling me to him very gently but persistently. It was a struggle for me to accept this calling and paradoxically I was feeling very much free to choose, free to accept this or not. I knew that whatever my choice of vocation was, God would still love me very much and this reality wouldn't change. It was a bit like having two doors open in front of me, each one opening to a path as luminous as the other and I had to choose one. I remember it vividly as I was in the kitchen and my mum was asking me if it was worth writing a cheque to continue my studies or not. I had a few seconds to choose and it seemed to me that I would be slightly happier in the consecrated life, so I stopped my studies and joined NDV. It is just looking back now that I realise it was the right choice."

4. How does God guide us and help us discern?

"Nothing is more practical than finding God, that is, than falling in love in a quite absolute, final way. What you are in love with, what seizes your imagination, will affect everything. It will decide what will get you out of bed in the morning, what you will do with your evenings, how you spend your weekends, what you read, who you know, what breaks your heart, and what amazes you with joy and gratitude. Fall in love, stay in love, and it will decide everything." (*Fr Pedro Arrupe SJ*)

The word 'discernment' is used to describe the whole process by which we listen to God and listen to our own hearts, gradually coming to know who God is calling us to be and where he is leading us. It is not something we just decide to do one afternoon, like baking a cake or watching a film. It is a journey that involves patience, honesty, perseverance, generosity, courage, and a sense of humour! It is a personal journey that will also involve trusted friends and the Christian community. Within all our discerning we are trying *to hear the invitation of Christ to follow him in a particular way and to become the person he wants us to be.*

Christians talk about how God 'calls' us to do something, and perhaps we think this means that one day we will literally hear a voice telling us what to do. Sometimes God does speak to us in clear and dramatic ways, but more often he 'speaks' to us in ordinary ways. He guides us *through the deepest desires of our hearts* (calling us 'from within') and *the events and circumstances of our lives* (calling us 'from without'). Later on in part 2 of this booklet there are sections about the particular signs that might point you to one vocation or another. This section, however, is simply a list of some of the many ways that God can guide you and pull you in a certain direction – whether it concerns a small choice, a medium-sized career move, or a lifelong commitment. Beneath everything, you are trying to know God's will for you, to listen to the stirrings of the Holy Spirit deep in your heart, and trying to respond generously. It is about a personal relationship with the Lord.

You don't need to over-analyse your life, looking for conclusive signs in every mood or event. This can become an obsession, and even a superstition, like reading the tea leaves or the horoscopes. The 'signs' listed here simply point to some areas of life that you can pay attention to, 'listening' to what they mean. *When you stand back and take a look at the big picture, perhaps a pattern emerges, and you sense that you are being drawn in a particular direction.* Usually, you don't really need more signs, you just need to look and listen more carefully.

Desire and attraction – What do you care about? What do you love? What do you feel passionate about? What would you love to commit yourself to? What do you feel pulled towards – even if you can't explain why?

Admiration – Which people do you admire the most? Is it because of who they are or what they stand for or what they do? *What is it about them or their vocation that you have been attracted to?* What does it stir up in your own heart? Which person, alive now, would you most like to be? Which saints, from the past, inspire you most? Why?

Enjoyment – What do you like doing; not just for leisure or fun – but what kind of work and activities do you enjoy most? Which bring the best out of you and gives you satisfaction at the end of a hard day?

Skills – What are you good at? What are your gifts and skills and aptitudes? Not just your qualifications (although these are often relevant) but your gifts of character and personality too. *How could you best use all that God has given you and make a difference?*

Value – Of the many projects and careers you are interested in, which of them are really worthwhile? Which allow you to contribute to something that is not just a waste of time? What do you actually believe in and want to promote? This doesn't mean you have to choose a 'religious' or 'charitable' work – as if all the ordinary jobs people do in the world are a second-best option for Christians, *but you have to have some sense that you believe in what you are doing.* Put it the other way round, you should avoid any choices that take you into an area that is corrupt or immoral, and above all avoid any wrongdoing yourself.

Events and circumstances – Sometimes an opportunity opens up unexpectedly and you want to make the most of it. It wasn't planned, and you are not quite sure how it fits into the rest of your life, but you feel an instinctive enthusiasm, and you want to 'seize the day'. Or you are waiting for an event to unfold that is now beyond your control: exam results, feedback from a job interview, a medical report. You may have a passionate desire to follow one path, but circumstances make it impossible. The Lord opens doors, and closes them, through the ordinary events of your life, through the decisions that others make, and through the concrete situation you are in. *You can trust that God is guiding all these circumstances and leading you to where you are meant to be.* He is more powerful than all the other forces that seem to be shaping your life.

Other people – If people encourage you in a particular decision or way of life, if they 'believe in you', this can be a sign that you are going in the right direction. *Sometimes other people can see your own potential more clearly than you can yourself.* You might be afraid or lacking confidence, but they can see the possibilities, and encourage you to go in one direction, or perhaps discourage you from going in another direction. It's good to talk to people that know you well, people you trust – friends, family, teachers, priests – and see what they think about your ideas for the future. They might have another perspective that helps you. But other people can also get things wrong, and become over-enthusiastic about your vocation, or project their own ideals onto your life – so you need to be cautious and not follow the advice someone else gives you uncritically.

Inner conviction – You might have *a clear, inner conviction that something is right for you*; almost like an unshakeable knowledge of who you are and what is important for you. More than just a desire or an attraction – it is like a sense of inevitability, part of your identity. It might have been a part of you for as long as you can remember; or it might have dawned slowly; or it might come upon you like a moment of inspiration. This inner conviction is not an infallible sign of your vocation – it might need interpreting or purifying – but it is certainly something that you should listen to carefully.

Ordinary prayer – When you are praying – talking to God, asking his help, or just sitting in silence – do certain ideas keep coming back to you? When you let go of your distractions for a moment, and open your heart to God in prayer, it can allow your deepest concerns to come to the surface, and allow the Lord to 'speak' to you. *Sometimes an idea comes to mind in prayer, or a memory, or a concern, or a task. It nags. It seems important, it seems especially meaningful.* And when you reflect on it later on, it still seems important for you. This might be an 'inspiration' from the Holy Spirit – not in the sense of an infallible divine command, but a nudge in your heart or mind to look into something more deeply.

Holy Scripture – In a similar way, when you are reading the bible alone, or listening to the scripture readings at Mass, *a phrase can strike you with unexpected force.* A passage that you have heard many times before can suddenly seem clear and powerful. It moves you or challenges you or almost impels you to do something. You feel as though God is speaking to you personally and directly through the words of the Bible, or through a sermon or talk. This is another way that the Holy Spirit can inspire and guide you – pointing you, through these words and the response they evoke, to something that is important for you.

Extraordinary experiences – Not often, but sometimes, *God steps into our life in a quite extraordinary and unexpected way.* You 'hear' a voice in prayer, or 'see' a vision, or witness a miracle – and you are quite convinced that this is God's direct work, and that he is speaking to you personally in this way, and guiding you in a certain direction or requesting something of you. You have to be very careful here: you can deceive yourself, and harmful spiritual forces can trick you into believing what is not true. You should never just trust these experiences uncritically – you should talk about them with a wise priest, and try to make sense of them in the light of all the other ways that God is guiding you. Many people do not have such experiences. We should not expect them, and there is no need to ask or pray for them. God usually prefers to guide us in ordinary ways. But sometimes it does happen!

Realism – Finally, you have to be realistic. You may have many desires and dreams, but they must grow out of who you are and what is possible for you at this time. This doesn't mean you should lack ambition and settle for second-best. It does mean, however, that *your thoughts about the future should be rooted in the reality of your life and of your situation.* You don't need to be defined by your weaknesses; but you do need to have the humility to accept your limitations, and a sincere gratitude for the person that God has created you to be.

Summary – God 'speaks' to us in all these different ways. Life is not like a crossword or a sudoku puzzle, where we have to analyse every clue and complete every answer in order to come to the end and reach a tidy conclusion. We simply get on with life, doing the best we can – 'listening' to God, paying attention to all these different areas listed above, seeing if there is a pattern, stopping to think when something strikes us with a new force or clarity. *Usually, gradually, we find that we are being pulled in a certain direction,* or we have enough to help us make a decision. And then we take the next step.

Fr Mark, Diocesan priest:

"My vocation story included the discernment of becoming a Catholic as well as the discernment of a priestly vocation. For me, the two went together. Since about the age of twelve I had people asking me whether I was considering ordination in the Church of

England. For whatever reason, and it may be that I was not listening sufficiently carefully to what God was asking, the answer was "No". The real catalyst was my parish priest posing the question, "Have you thought about priesthood?" and suggesting that I should – quite seriously. The greatest aids to discernment were his priestly example and advice, prayer and the sacraments, and seeing a spiritual director. I was so shocked by the initial approach from the priest, that I chose not to talk to others about the possibility for the next few months. I was surprised, therefore, to be asked on numerous occasions during that time by people from all areas of my life whether I was thinking of priesthood. Perhaps there was something to be investigated after all."

Elizabeth, wife and mother:

"When I was a bored teenager, we moved next door to a sick woman who was glad to let me take her babies for walks. There was a feeling inside me that I was meant to be a mother, in marriage. No other life occurred to me. I was not Catholic, and had never met a nun. Later on, I moved to London, and met my husband through work, at a social event. We were both Christian, and both musical. When we eventually married, life was all joy. Within a few months I discovered the Catholic Church, and knew that God was calling me to enter. There were some tensions about that, but we loved one another deeply, and we both loved children. It seems like a miracle to us that we have produced three beloved children, despite three early miscarriages. In difficult times, it was daily prayer and the sacraments, that kept me going. My husband is now a Catholic. Through God's kindness we have a peaceful home for our children, grandchildren, neighbours and friends."

5. What can I do to be more open to my vocation?

"Take, O Lord, and receive: all my liberty, my memory, my understanding, and my entire will. All I have and all I possess are yours, Lord. You have given it all to me. Now I return it to you. Dispose of it according to your will. Give me only your love and your grace, for this is enough for me." (*St Ignatius of Loyola*)

If you are not clear about your vocation, what can you do? Let's say you are working or studying – how can you make the most of this time? How can you listen more and let God work in your life more? You cannot force things; and you should be patient. Perhaps the Lord does not want to give you an answer now, and you just need to live your ordinary life as faithfully as you can. But if you are serious about discerning your vocation, then there are certain things you can do. Here are some tips.

Give your life to God – Just say to him, perhaps in your own words, '*I am completely yours, I give you everything. I will do whatever you ask of me.* I give you all my fears and doubts. Show me your will, and I will follow it. I am yours'. Say this as a prayer, and really mean it. This is the only way you will find true freedom; and only if you are free can he call you. He will not let you down; he won't ask you to do something that is wrong for you, or that you are unable to fulfil. *All he wants is your willingness and openness.* This is the first and most fundamental part of being a Christian; and it's the first and most basic part of discovering your vocation. If you can't say it, you will always be fighting or missing something. This is simply the prayer of the Our Father: 'Thy will be done'. We just need to mean it when we say it.

✳ **Live your Catholic Faith** – Make sure you are living the basics that any Catholic should be living: *going to Mass each Sunday; praying each day; trying to keep the commandments; going to confession regularly; loving your neighbour as best you can.* Now and then you may be able to go to Mass during the week as well as Sunday; or visit a Catholic Church and pray in front of the Blessed Sacrament.

✓ **Deepen your prayer life** – Don't go mad, as if you can force God to give you an answer by praying all the time. But deepen your prayer life, and develop a routine. *Set aside some time each day,* perhaps just five or ten minutes. *Have at least some quiet time to reflect and listen.* Read the scriptures, especially the Gospels, prayerfully – notice what attracts you, what speaks to you. Have some time just to talk to the Lord, to ask for his help – talk to him with complete honesty. Pray to Our Lady, maybe the rosary, maybe just a decade, or whatever prayers you are attracted to – entrust your life and your vocation to her. Pray to the saints, especially those who have lived the vocation you are thinking about. At the end of each day look back on what has happened, thank God for the good things that have happened, and say sorry for any sins you have committed. *It is good to make one specific prayer each day for the intention that God will help you to discover your vocation.* It can be a set prayer about vocation; or it can simply be to pray the Our Father or Hail Mary for that intention.

Create some space in your life for silence – You don't need to go off and live in a monastery for a year, but you do need to have at least some silence and quiet time in your week – *to let go of all the activity, to get some perspective on life*, and to listen to your own heart. It might be a few moments in your room at the end of the day, or popping into a church during the week, or simply going for a walk in the park.

Grow in holiness – Be really honest with yourself about your faults and sins. Be really determined to live a life of holiness. If there are habits of sin in your life, face up to them, make a decision to begin anew. If there is something in your way of life that is making it difficult to live a good life, be honest about it, and make some changes. You are called to be a saint, to find happiness in a life of goodness and holiness, and you can't find it if you are clinging to some sin or unhealthy lifestyle. *Often the Lord can't speak to you, or you can't hear him, if you are not sincerely trying to live a Christian life.* If you are committed to your faith and discerning seriously, you should also try to go to confession regularly, e.g. every month.

Live a life of service – Part of your discernment can be making a decision to love and serve others in your ordinary life at work or college or wherever you are, and perhaps to take on some commitment to serve others in your free time, some voluntary work or work in the parish. *This desire to be kind and generous will actually help your discernment and deepen your vocation.* It is part of the way Christ makes us more like him, the way he expands our hearts. Every vocation is a call to love, so the more you can grow in an active love for your neighbour, the more you can be prepared for your vocation – whatever it is. Your experience of service will also help you to discover the best side of yourself, and will open up the deepest desires that God has planted in your heart, below the superficial worries and attractions. And if you are discerning your vocation you can easily become obsessed with yourself, so it is good just to look outwards towards others and forget yourself for a while.

Live a life of chastity – To make a proper decision about vocation you need to have a free and generous heart, and one of the struggles that can ensnare our hearts in a particular way is the struggle with chastity. Chastity is not just about avoiding immoral behaviour – it is far more about learning to love in a way that will bring you true happiness; it is about living your relationships and sexuality in a way that respects the deepest meaning of love. *It will keep your love pure, unpossessive and free.* So in your personal life, try to have a pure heart and a pure mind; and be modest and chaste in your relationships. Above all, remember that sexual intimacy and sex itself are meant to be an expression of the complete love between a husband and wife, and outside of marriage they can only distort and even damage love – and make true friendship and discernment much harder.

Find some good spiritual reading – Have a book that you can dip into every day or two: *find something that inspires you* about the Christian faith or prayer or the Bible; something about the vocation you are considering. Read about the lives of the saints; about what the Church believes; about how to pray. Read a little bit every day, and at least something every week. Don't force yourself to read something that you don't like – if a book isn't helping and inspiring you, then move on and find something else. *Just make sure that it is spiritually nourishing for you.*

Join a Catholic group – Any good group! It doesn't matter whether it is a vocations discernment group, or a parish prayer group, or a bible study group, or a young-adult socialising group. The main thing is to make sure that you are *not living your faith alone*, and that you have other people around to encourage you, to help you see that you are not the only person living your faith and exploring your direction in life.

Talk honestly with someone you trust – *At some stage you need to talk about your sense of vocation and not just keep it to yourself.* You might not find the perfect guide, but just try and think of someone who is wise and prayerful and faithful to the Church. It might be your parish priest, or another priest you know; it might be a wise layperson in the parish or somewhere else. You might call them your 'spiritual director', but the title is not important. It is good to have one-off conversations; but it is also good to have someone you can talk with over time, coming back to things; who can give advice and give an outside opinion; and can help you see some patterns in your faith and vocation that emerge over a period of time.

Fr Matthew, Jesuit priest:
"A crucial part of my own vocation story was to have powerful experiences of Christian community at a time when I was wondering what God was calling me to. Three in particular stand out: spending a week in the summer, over a period of four years, working with friends looking after disabled and socially disadvantaged children – we had Mass everyday and prayed together in the evening. Then there were two Holy Weeks when I walked from Chichester to Worth Abbey over the South Downs, carrying a cross. Finally, I remember with gratitude a week spent at Taizé. I often hear people saying that to discover your vocation you need to uncover your deepest desires. And I tend to agree. But there are many things we desire in life, there

are many things that cry out to us 'choose me'. What I found in the experiences mentioned above was a slow growing into freedom brought about by the love and support of others, a love and support that made it possible for me to be more open to look beneath and beyond my neediness and to hear more clearly the Lord's invitation to follow him."

Sr Cathy, Religious of the Assumption:

"Between the ages of 16 to 25 I often wondered whether God was calling me to religious life. During this time I was studying theology, and an answer to my vocational questioning came unexpectedly, as I read a rather dull commentary on the Canon Law of the Church. The description of religious life spoke powerfully to me and from that moment on, I was clear about my call to religious life. The next step was to find which order to join. I was particularly attracted by Franciscan simplicity, so decided that I would become a Franciscan. However, God had other plans. As I visited various Franciscan orders I kept thinking of the Religious of the Assumption whom I had worked with for a few years, during my studies. I'd been a care-assistant looking after the very elderly sisters, in particular one saintly sister, who had severe dementia, but who radiated the love of God. At the time I hadn't thought of joining the sisters as they were all quite old, but God slowly broke down my resistances, mainly through the powerful memories of this very frail sister. Eight years later I am very thankful to God for having led me here, and I hope that one day, I too will be a saintly old sister."

6. How do I make a decision?

"Above all trust in the slow work of God. We are, quite naturally, impatient in everything to reach the end without delay. We should like to skip the intermediate stages. We are impatient of being on the way to something unknown, something new. And yet it is the law of all progress that it is made by passing through some stages of instability – and that it may take a very long time.

And so I think it is with you. Your ideas mature gradually – let them grow, let them shape themselves, without undue haste. Don't try to force them on, as though you could be today what time (that is to say, grace and circumstances acting on your good will) will make you tomorrow.

Only God could say what this new spirit gradually forming within you will be. Give our Lord the benefit of believing that his hand is leading you, and accept the anxiety of feeling yourself in suspense and incomplete." (*Fr Pierre Teilhard de Chardin SJ*)

Usually our vocation becomes clearer over time. If you are living your Catholic faith, and being open to the Lord and to all that is happening in your life, you should gradually feel a pull in one direction, a growing conviction that one way of life is right for you. This process of discernment takes time, and it is much more than simply trying to make practical decisions.

Yet there are two reasons why you might come to a time in your life when you need to make a decision of some kind. First, *because things have become clearer*, and you feel you are ready to take a step in a certain direction. Second, *because things are not at all clear,* and you have been going round in circles about your vocation for a long time, and you don't seem to be getting anywhere. In this case it can be helpful, with the support of a wise person you trust, to try and make some kind of provisional decision about where you are going. There is a risk that you could drift through life without making any decisions; always looking for signs that will tell you what to do, without actively taking responsibility for your own choices. You could become a 'serial discerner' and fall prey to 'paralysis through analysis'.

Sometimes God lays before us different possibilities, and wants us to come to a decision about what seems best thoughtfully and prayerfully. It is not a *final* decision (we don't make a final decision until the day of our marriage or ordination or solemn profession), it is simply a decision to test the water instead of hovering at the edge, to start down one particular path instead of standing at the crossroads. *We shouldn't be surprised that God sometimes invites us to make a choice.* Sometimes, but not always, we learn more about God and about ourselves by acting than by waiting. We are often looking for certainty, for objective signs. *But one of the 'signs' of a vocation can be our willingness to try a particular path and see where it leads.* He leads us partly through our choices. You don't have to be certain about the choice, you just have to make the best choice that you can. If you wait for 100% certainty you will be waiting forever.

Here are some tips about how to make a decision when the time comes. You don't need to use them all, like a checklist – they are simply ideas in case you are stuck.

Wait – God's call usually becomes clearer over time. Often we just need to wait patiently – living our Catholic faith, doing all we can to be open to God's will, praying for his help and guidance. Don't force the issue. Something will happen – in your own heart, or in the circumstances of your life.

Weigh up the pros and cons – Take some extra time to reflect on your life and on all the factors that seem significant in this choice. What are the options before you? Write down the pros and cons of each option. Think about them. Weigh them up. Put the list away and come back to it a few days later. *What seems to be most important for you? What seems best?*

Imagine you have made a decision – It can sometimes help to imagine that we have made one particular choice (and then to imagine that we have made an alternative choice). Be very concrete. *Imagine telling your friends and family; imagine taking the next step.* Imagine changing your life accordingly. Imagine where you will be in a few weeks, a few months. *What feelings does this stir up? What hopes and fears?* Excitement? Relief? Despondency? Regret? These feelings can sometimes reveal what is deep in our heart. Another idea is to imagine you are at the very end of your life, looking back on all that might have happened as you followed this path. Can you be proud of such a life and pleased to offer it to God? Or would you be disappointed or sad?

Talk to someone – Not just anyone, not just a friend who will say what you want to hear. It should be someone you trust, a committed Catholic, who is wise, and who will be honest with you. It might be a friend or relation or a priest you know; or someone you don't know who has been recommended by, for example, your parish priest. They might give you some good advice and encouragement. But even if they don't say much it is *enormously valuable to talk about our hopes and fears in this way.* It forces us to put into words the vague thoughts and feelings we have; and it gives us new courage and clarity simply because we have been brave enough to open our heart to another person – our hopes and worries about vocation are no longer just a 'secret', they become more real, more urgent.

Pray – Pray to God for guidance and help. Pray especially to the Holy Spirit for wisdom. *Make a particular prayer each day for help as you make this* *decision.* If you are about to make a big decision, *ask a priest to offer Mass for your own personal intentions* (which are that you will make a good decision – you don't have to explain all this to him). To offer Mass for an intention in this way brings great graces to any situation. *But don't pray too much!* Sometimes, especially if you are feeling desperate, you might think that you have to pray more and more, as if you are forcing God's hand. It can become a kind of superstition, and you half-worry that God will not help you unless you pray for hours every day and turn your life upside down with devotions. This is simply not true. God loves you and cares for you and wants the best for you. He certainly wants you to pray, but in whatever way is right for you as a layperson studying or working in the world.

Listen to your heart – Sometimes, when we make time to think about one course of action or one possibility, it brings with it *a deep sense of peace and joy; not just a passing mood or emotion, but an inner feeling that something is right, a contentment and quiet excitement, a sense of reassurance and freedom, of being on the right track*. At other times, when we stop to reflect in this way, an idea brings with it feelings of fear and panic and worry and insecurity; a sense of heaviness and imposition and unnecessary obligation. *The spiritual peace (or 'consolation') can be a sign that one path is right for us, a sign that it fits with who we are and who*

God calls us to be. The fear and panic (or 'desolation') can be a sign that one path is not right for us, that it is pulling us away from who we are and who God calls us to be. But some fears and doubts (see the chapter 7 below), natural fears that we are bound to face when we make big decisions, are not signs of anything deep – and they simply need to be faced and overcome.

Take a single step – If you are still unsure what to do and feel paralysed and unable to make a big decision, it can help to make a small decision instead. *Decide to take just one step down a certain path, the next step – so that you can see how it feels and how it turns out.* You don't need to find certainty that this is the final step for you; you simply need to have some confidence that it is a good and worthwhile step in itself at this moment. For example: if you have never talked to anyone about your dilemmas, then decide to talk to someone. If you are unsure about a vocation to the priesthood, then at least go and speak to your vocations director. If you are fond of someone but unsure about marriage, then at least try to get to know them better. If you would love to be a nun, but feel pulled in different directions, then make a decision to visit a convent and even arrange to stay for a few days. If you are seriously considering a vocation to the priesthood or the religious life, but are still unsure of how to find certainty – then why not consider making an application and see how you feel? You can always change your mind in the next few weeks. Or you can leave after the first few months. Often simply making one decision helps us to see that it is the wrong decision – and nothing is lost, but great clarity is gained. Or perhaps you won't be accepted, and that will certainly be a sign that this is not for you.

Make a decision – The English language is instructive. We don't *find* a decision – we make one. Sometimes we imagine that a vocation is something we have to find: if I can only *find* the answer, read the signs, discover the path – then I will happily walk along it. There is some truth to this, and the title of this booklet is all about 'discovering' your vocation. But as well as this, *a vocation is also something you have to choose.* With all the signs in front of you, with all that lies in your own heart, there is a moment when you will need to weigh everything up and simply make a decision. Not a final decision you are certain about, but the best decision possible at this time – a 'provisional' decision. Looking for infallible signs can paradoxically be a way of avoiding the responsibility and risk of making a decision.

There are not many moments of decision like this, but there are some. *You can trust that God will help you to make a wise decision now; and above all that his plan for your life will unfold through the consequences of your prayerful decision.* If it is the 'wrong' provisional decision, and you are meant to be somewhere else – he will make that clear before too long. If it is the 'right' provisional decision, and you are meant to continue along this road – he will confirm that for you and make it clearer and clearer. Only when you are at the stage of making lifelong promises or vows will he ask you to make an irrevocable decision – and by that stage you will have had many reassurances that this is the right path for you.

Trust in Providence – Above all, you can trust in God's Providence. If you are not yet at the point of making decisions, then trust that God will guide and enlighten you. If you are about to make an important decision, trust that God will help you to make a wise one. If you have made a decision, trust that God will lead you to know if it is indeed the right one. He loves you more than you love yourself. He cares for you with an unbounded tenderness and affection. His power is greater than any other force in creation, and his Providence is guiding everything and will put right even the mistakes you may make. So be at peace. Do all that you can; but trust in the Lord.

Fr Simon, Jesuit priest:
"I first thought of becoming a priest when I was thirteen years old. A Jesuit priest had invited me and six other friends to start a prayer group, going through the Gospel of St Mark week by week. It was as if a light bulb inside me was suddenly turned on. That experience of following Jesus, of seeing how he lived and prayed, of how he loved across boundaries, physical, cultural, moral, spiritual, made me say, "I want to live my life like that." I then spent the next twelve years trying to run away from this

desire: "This is mad"; "This is impossible"; "I can't do it". I found myself arguing with God: "Can't I get married, create a family, and be a good, faithful Catholic." It took some time, with the help of daily prayer, regular spiritual direction and a couple of retreats to realise that I was, in fact, pushing against an open door. God did not mind if I chose to be married or to remain single or to become a religious and/or a priest, what he wanted was for me to be his, to live my life with him, whatever way I lived that out. That was the first and most important vocation. I was still not 100% sure and a wise Jesuit said to me: "It seems you have done all that you can reasonably do: you have been praying daily, you have been meeting a spiritual director regularly, you have made a couple of retreats, you have met different priests and religious congregations and it seems to you that you are being led in a particular direction. What I suggest for your prayer is that, instead of continuing to wonder endlessly what you should do, say to the Lord: 'Lord, it seems to me, after all my praying, discussing, meeting and discerning, you are calling me in this direction. That's the direction I'm going to take, so if it's not the correct road, you're going to have to torpedo me!'" So I remember saying to myself, 'This may not be for me, but I'll give it a go, and if it's not right, I'm sure that will become obvious, to me and to the others in the community, and then I can leave happily, knowing that it's not for me.' I was so surprised, then, walking into my small, bare room in the Jesuit novitiate that I had this overwhelming sense of peace, of joy and of freedom – I had come home! This is where not only God wanted me to be, but where I, too, wanted to be. God didn't torpedo me!"

7. What can get in the way?

"My Lord God, I have no idea where I am going. I do not see the road ahead of me. I cannot know for certain where it will end. Nor do I really know myself, and the fact that I think I am following your will does not mean that I am actually doing so.

But I believe that the desire to please you does in fact please you and I hope that I have that desire in all that I am doing. I hope that I will never do anything apart from that desire. And I know that if I do this, you will lead me by the right road, though I may know nothing about it.

Therefore will I trust you always though I may seem to be lost and in the shadow of death. I will not fear, for you are ever with me and you will never leave me to face my struggles alone." (*Thomas Merton*)

Many factors can get in the way of our vocation; they can make it difficult to discern or difficult to make a commitment once we have discerned. There is no space here to look carefully at all these difficulties. Sometimes it is enough just to flag them up, so that if they are present in your life you can notice them more easily and face them more honestly. Here are some of the common difficulties that arise when people are discerning their vocation, together with a single thought about each one to encourage you or help you. If you meet a real difficulty, pray about it, and talk to someone about it, so it does not become an insurmountable obstacle.

Worry, anxiety – Try not to worry. Be at peace. *Trust that God is more powerful than all your worries.* Tell him your honest anxieties, and put them in his loving hands.

Lack of trust – You may have a distorted image of God. You may think he is like an absent parent who doesn't love you, or a kind uncle who will never make any demands on you, or a vengeful tyrant who is punishing you for something, or an unpredictable boss who wants to force you into a vocation that will not be right for you. Instead, *trust him. He is a tender Father who is both loving and demanding.* He cares for you more than you care for yourself. Sometimes he might challenge you and call you to something unexpected – but it will always be for your ultimate good and happiness.

Noise, busyness, overwork – Perhaps you can't hear God's call because you never make any space to listen to him. Every hour is full up, and your mind is constantly cluttered with work, noise, music, and other distractions. *Make space for God and for at least some moments of silence in each day.*

Not praying, not living your faith – You will never know yourself properly or know the call of the Lord if you are not making some space for prayer each day and trying to live your Catholic faith.

Sin, worldliness – If you are trapped in some habitual sin or caught up in a completely worldly lifestyle, it may be impossible to listen to your own heart or to God. *Be* *honest with yourself;* go to confession; try to make a new start even if you are still struggling.

Addictive behaviours – Alcohol, drugs, pornography, sex, gambling; even activities that are harmless in themselves like work, sport, texting, the internet, gaming, Facebook – they can become like addictions that cover up our deepest needs and cut us off from true selves. *Try and break any addictive patterns of behaviour you are trapped in.* And if you can't – then get help.

Avoiding the question of vocation – If the question of vocation is nagging at you, don't just run away from it. It will come back whether you like it or not! And in the meantime you will make yourself more and more unhappy. *So face it honestly,* in prayer and in conversations with someone you trust.

Fear of commitment – We rightly value freedom, but in the Western world we confuse freedom with being able to choose from an endless variety of options. Commitment to anything, let alone for life, seems like a limitation, even a loss of oneself. *But to have a series of endless options is actually to have no options* – because you never embrace any one of them with your whole heart. *God may be inviting you to make a lifelong commitment, to put down roots so that you can truly flourish,* to build one concrete life rather than to fantasise about innumerable possible lives, to take responsibility for your own life. It is sometimes better to do one thing with your unreserved commitment than to drift through life without any firm sense of purpose.

Desire for certainty – It's unlikely that you will ever be 100% certain about any significant choice – of course there are doubts and questions. But *you can be sure enough that this is a reasonable step to take,* when things come together and the time is right. Yes, it's a risk. But it's also a risk not to make a choice. Life is full of risks. God is always with us, supporting and guiding us – even if we make a decision in good faith and things seem to go wrong.

Fear of your own inadequacy – Perhaps you fear you are not the right person for this vocation, even though you feel attracted to it. You worry that you are not holy enough, not intelligent enough, not qualified enough, not loving enough, too shy, too sociable... Perhaps you are right. *But perhaps you are underestimating yourself or underestimating God. He chooses the weak and makes them strong.* Sometimes he invites us to do what seems impossible, and only later on gives us the strength to do it. Why not take a step anyway – and let God decide further down the line if it is really not for you.

Attachment to personal ambition or lifestyle – Any lifelong commitment will involve some sacrifice and cost, giving up something you are attached to now (lifestyle, habits, income, pleasures, people), letting go of what could have been (freedom, dreams, ambitions). Sometimes we have to move on – it's inevitable. *Trust* *that if this is really your vocation, it will be a treasure that will be worth any sacrifice,* and that God will 'reimburse' you in other unexpected ways. Remember that our minds usually exaggerate the difficulties; and God will help you to deal with the ones that remain. And be honest if the real reason you are reluctant to follow your vocation is simply selfishness.

Fear of failure – If this is the right step for you, then God will sustain you. If he wants you to flourish and find happiness here, then you will. If he is actually leading you somewhere else, and it seems like you have failed in your provisional decision to try a vocation – then trust that this will be part of his loving plan. He writes straight with crooked lines. *What matters is not success or failure, but whether you have tried to be faithful to his call at each moment.*

Conflicting desires – You are trying to listen to your heart, but you find that there are many conflicting desires there, and not one of them seems to be more important than the others. Then follow the advice in chapter 6 above: pray, wait for as long as you need to, and if everything is still unclear, then take a step in one direction just to test the water. The Lord will gradually show you whether this is the right step or whether you should go back and try another.

Desire for perfection – Perhaps you want to be a religious brother or sister but you can't find an order that is good enough for you; you want to be a Diocesan priest but don't like the bishop in your Diocese; you want to be married but no-one matches up to your standards. It may be that you haven't found the right person or diocese or congregation yet; but *it may be that you need to settle for what is 'good enough'*. No person or congregation is perfect, and if you are looking for perfection you will never find it. *The search for perfection might strangely be a way of avoiding a vocation.* Try the 80% rule: if 80% of what you are looking at is good – then that's pretty good! Perhaps you can live with the other 20%, or see it in a new light, or change it.

Age – You fear you are too old to get married or become a priest or consecrated person. You fear you have missed the boat. But the Lord wants you to accept that this is the age you are. Give thanks to God for who you are and where you are, instead of regretting what has not happened in the past. *If you are pulled towards a certain vocation, whatever your age, then take a step and test that vocation. If God wants you to follow it, he will make things possible.*

Opposition from people you love – Your family or friends are against you taking this step. It may be true that they have some insight that you don't have, and you should certainly listen to them respectfully. But it may be that they are unable to support you in your vocation because of their own lack of faith or personal fears. *Sometimes you need to be strong and do what you feel is right, even in the face of opposition or misunderstanding.*

If you have carefully discerned that this is the right step, then explain it as best you can to those you love, and take it courageously – trusting that God will help them to understand or at least to accept it some time in the future.

Opposition from the culture and society – Some vocational choices, even Christian marriage, will sometimes be misunderstood or mocked by contemporary society, and perhaps by friends or colleagues. Recognise that *to be a Christian will involve some misunderstanding and even persecution,* especially if you make a lifelong vocational commitment. Be as loving and kind as you can, and explain your choices gently to people if they ask. *Don't stir up opposition and seek controversy. But if it comes, don't be deterred.*

A long-term relationship that is drifting – If you have been dating someone for a long time, and the relationship is not deepening and drawing you in the direction of marriage, and if you are in effect going out with someone simply for the sake of it – this can make your own discernment of vocation very difficult. The relationship is taking up your time and emotional energy and taking away your freedom to discern properly. You can't be properly open to other vocations; you can't even be open to meeting other people. Even though there may be a real love and commitment between you both, if you are drifting, then it is usually better to *make a proper decision about marriage, or draw things to an end* – so that each of you can be free to discover what is God's plan for you.

Fear of not having a family – If you are considering priesthood or consecrated life then you may well be anxious about the idea of not having a husband or wife and a family. This is quite understandable. And perhaps you should indeed get married! But this anxiety might stem partly from the fear that a celibate life will be a life without love. You need to believe two things. First, *the celibate life is a life full of love* – of the intimate love of Christ, and the love of all those you will meet and work with and live with. And you will, God willing, discover an aspect of 'spiritual fatherhood' or 'spiritual motherhood' in your vocation – loving and nurturing those in your care – that will be deeply fulfilling. But second, *there are certainly sacrifices made in a life of celibacy*, not least in letting go of the possibility of the love of marriage and family. But there are also huge sacrifices made in marriage, and sometimes much loneliness. The cost of loving is high in any Christian vocation. *What matters is that you find what is right for you – and trust that God will give you all the love you need, through prayer and through others, to sustain you in this vocation.*

Jo, a young woman still discerning:
"Vocation is deeply mysterious. To discover and embrace God's call is to take a step each day into the unknown, carving out the

path to God that is uniquely mine. The invitation has been to patience and trust, struggling to reach a point where I can say 'one step enough for me' – not in control of the future, nor with inside knowledge as to where God may be leading, but simply open and listening, trying to say with as much of me as will consent at any time, 'Here I am Lord. I'm coming to obey your will.' My journey continues. I am tentatively feeling a way forward in the dark. Over the last five years, I've strained quite a lot for certainty about my future, to know the way ahead. But I've learned it doesn't work like that. We don't know the particulars of where we will be led if we say 'yes' to Christ. He invites us to say 'I will follow you' before we know where he is heading."

Rod, husband and father:

"For me the big struggle was to wade through the layers of fear, insecurity and ambivalence about both priesthood and marriage until I had reached a certain freedom to hear God's invitation. I spent ages looking for my vocation and ages praying about it, but I think I only began to discover it when I started to really look for God instead. Jean Vanier helped me a lot simply by saying, "Rod, I think the question is not so much priesthood or marriage or single life, but 'Do you really want to follow Jesus?'" I was irritated at the time. I thought, 'Of course I do. I've become a Catholic haven't I?' But he was spot on. I was partly afraid of God and partly afraid of myself. And asking Ann Marie to marry me was all about feeling the fear and knowing that I could offer my life to God and to her. It wasn't easy. It felt a bit like stepping off the edge of a cliff. But at the same time, there was a sense of peace that came as soon as I had made the decision. Of course, it helped that she said 'Yes' when I asked her!"

II. SIGNS OF A PARTICULAR VOCATION

8. What are the signs that God might be calling me to marriage?

"If we let Christ enter fully into our lives, if we open ourselves totally to him, are we not afraid that he might take something away from us? Are we not perhaps afraid to give up something significant, something unique, something that makes life so beautiful? Do we not then risk ending up diminished and deprived of our freedom? Pope John Paul said: No! If we let Christ into our lives, we lose nothing, nothing, absolutely nothing of what makes life free, beautiful and great. No! Only in this friendship are the doors of life opened wide. Only in this friendship is the great potential of human existence truly revealed. Only in this friendship do we experience beauty and liberation. And so, today, with great strength and great conviction, on the basis of long personal experience of life, I say to you, dear young people: Do not be afraid of Christ! He takes nothing away, and he gives you everything. When we give ourselves to him, we receive a hundredfold in return. Yes, open, open wide the doors to Christ – and you will find true life." (*Pope Benedict XVI*)

Marriage could be called a 'natural' vocation. God, who is love, has created us in his own image and likeness, and planted in our hearts a longing to love and be loved. And it is perfectly natural that as men and women we should want this love to be fulfilled in the love of marriage – a love that is without reservation, faithful, lifelong, and open to new life. When this marriage is between two Christians it is transformed into a sacrament, and the natural and God-given call to marriage becomes something far, far deeper – a joyful and costly call to follow Christ and to give one's life in love, in the context of marriage and family.

Not everyone wants to get married, and not everyone who hopes to marry does actually get married. But if someone freely chooses to get married it does not usually need a lot of explaining. *The reasons are straightforward: a desire for love and family and children that grows out of who we are as human beings, as men and women.* For Christians who are discerning marriage there will be deeper vocational questions: listening to Christ, listening to the deepest desires of your heart, reflecting on the unique person you are called to be and on the particular ways you hope to give your life in love and service. *Christian marriage is a sacrament, a vocation, and if you choose to be married it will be a sign of your love for Christ as much as of your love for another person.* But it is not the kind of call that pulls you away from your natural hopes and expectations. Marriage is not easier to live than other vocations, but it is easier to explain. If you long to be married, and there are no other big pulls in your life, then you should be at peace about seeking a husband or wife.

Here are some signs that might show you are called to be married. As with any signs, they need to be interpreted carefully, and understood in the context of your whole life and all that is happening to you. This is not a checklist of essential requirements, it is simply an indication of some of the ways that God might be guiding you in your life. The overall pattern and the deepest pulls will show you which direction is right for you.

A desire to be married – Perhaps you have always wanted to be married. The desire was there when you were a child, and it has never left you. Or as you have grown older, and thought more about vocation and the future, *you realise that above all else you would love to be married*. You imagine yourself as a husband or wife and it brings you great peace and joy. You long to love someone and to be loved by them, and to make that love the centre of your life and vocation.

A desire to have children – *You would love to have a family, to have children of your own*. Despite all the difficulties and sacrifices of raising children, the desire is there deep in your heart. You can imagine yourself being a father or mother, taking on that role in different ways, relating to your children in all their different stages of life. When you think of yourself as a parent, even if there is some trepidation, it comes with a sense of peace and excitement. But you also have to remember that children are a gift to a couple, and there is no guarantee that you will have children even if you get married. What matters is that you are open to this gift: open in your heart before you get married, and open to new life in your sexual union after you get married.

An admiration for husbands or wives and fathers or mothers that you know – You admire others who are married. Not necessarily everyone, but there are some husbands or wives, fathers or mothers, that have made a real impression on you. They seem happy and fulfilled, despite the struggles. *They seem to have discovered a love that you wish you had, and a way of living their Christian faith that inspires you.* They seem to be living a life that is worthwhile. You can see yourself being happy in their shoes.

Other people encourage you towards marriage – When you chat with people you trust, people who know you well, it seems perfectly natural to them that you might get married. If the subject comes up, even if half-jokingly, they encourage you, and say that you would be a good husband or wife, a good father or mother. *They think you could be happy in this life*; and there are no warning bells ringing for them suggesting that you should be doing something else instead. Other people are not infallible – but they might have a good sense of what is right for you.

You meet someone you want to marry – Often the call to marriage is not a 'theory', an abstract desire, it is a concrete person. Perhaps you don't have a strong desire to get married, and there isn't a general longing for children, but *you meet someone and fall in love and everything changes. The abstract idea of marriage suddenly becomes very real.* You love someone and through the strength of that love realise that you want to be with them for the rest of your life, to share your life *with them* completely, and to have children *with them*. The love of a real person helps you discern your Christian vocation. Love in itself, love alone, despite what many think, is not a good enough reason to get married. There are many other factors that need weighing up, not least whether a couple have the same understanding of marriage, and whether they are really suitable for each other. *But meeting the right person can sometimes be the catalyst that helps you to understand what your deepest desire is and what God is calling you to.*

There are no other big pulls in your life – On its own, of course, the absence of another vocation is not a reason to get married. But if there are no signs of a vocation to the priesthood or the consecrated life then this sets us free, as it were, to look into marriage and to believe that it might be the right vocation for us.

Sophie, wife and mother:

"I was lucky to always have had quite an open mind about my future. I had had positive experiences of both married life and religious or consecrated life and I could see the benefits of both. When it came to my personal life journey, I think my chosen vocation (to be married) was something that came out of waiting patiently to hear what God was saying to me and also being ready to respond once the right person came along. So waiting, discerning and responding, I would say are the key elements. Before getting engaged and then married, I had never had a serious boyfriend or anything like that, but I think many years of single life and years of deepening my own relationship with God contributed to my understanding of the importance of a relationship once it happened. I mean to say that I didn't spend years of my life planning out what kind of person I would marry, but I think unconsciously, I knew what I wanted … and what I didn't want, based on indirect experiences of others and also a deepening of my own faith! I knew that the most important thing for me was to find someone I could trust in and who loved me for who I am and someone that I could love whole-heartedly, but also someone who had the same thirst for God in their lives. Finally I would say vocation is about making a decision. A decision based, in part, on common sense and an informed understanding, but also one made in faith."

9. How can I find a good husband or wife?

"Lord, may I grow in consideration towards others, honesty with myself, and faithfulness to you. Make me generous enough to want sincerely to do your will whatever it may be. Help me to find my true vocation in life, and grant that through it I may find happiness myself and bring happiness to others. Grant, Lord, that those whom you call to a particular vocation may have the generosity to answer your call, so that those who need your help may always find it. We ask this through Christ our Lord." (*Author unknown; adapted*)

Most young people hope to get married and have children one day. *The clearest sign that marriage is for you is simply that you have a desire to get married and have a family, and you do not have a sense of being pulled towards another vocation.* If this is the case then it is perfectly reasonable to hope that you will be married, and to pray that God will help you to find a good husband or wife.

There are many happy and holy marriages between Catholics and non-Catholics, but if you are a Catholic *it is a real blessing if you can find a husband or wife who shares your faith.* This means that you will have the same Catholic values and the same understanding of the deepest meaning of marriage; that you can support each other in the practice of your own faith; and that you can have a shared understanding of how to bring up your children in the Catholic faith. Here are some tips on finding such a husband or wife. It is not wrong or unreasonable to consider marrying someone who is not Catholic; but it is certainly worth hoping and praying that you will meet someone who is a committed Catholic.

Pray every day that God will lead you to a good husband or wife – Just say a short, simple prayer for that intention every day; use your own words, or say a 'formal' prayer for this intention such as the Our Father or Hail Mary. You can even do this if you are young and not thinking about marriage yet. And pray to the Virgin Mary and to St Joseph for this intention.

Find out more about the Catholic vision of marriage – Our ideas about marriage are formed by so many different influences: by our family background, by friends, by the media, etc. Some of our ideas will be good and healthy, but some of them might be distorted or wrong. It will be a great help if you can *find out more about the true Catholic vision of marriage* – above all by reading. This vision will inspire you to seek a good Catholic husband or wife; it will help you to look for the right things in a relationship; and it will prepare you in a realistic way for the great challenge of married life.

Be a good person yourself – The best way to meet a good person, a person of faith, is to be a good person yourself, to be a person of faith. *Like attracts like*. That person is looking for someone full of love and goodness too. So live your faith. Live a life of prayer and love. Be the best person you can be. *And this will help you to meet the right person and to build the best relationship you can.*

Socialise with other Catholics – You don't have to socialise *only* with other Catholics, *but if you want to meet a Catholic husband or wife, make sure you are actually meeting some other Catholics*. Go to Catholic youth events, prayer groups, retreats, pilgrimages – anything at all! Use Facebook and other social networking websites to hook into Catholic groups and events in your area. If you feel comfortable with it, perhaps use a Catholic online dating website. You have to be cautious meeting people online, but it might be that you can discover a wider range of practising Catholics on a Catholic website than you can in your ordinary social life.

Don't date just for the sake of it – There is often a lot of pressure on people to be in a relationship. It can come from your peer group, or from society, and it makes you feel that life is empty and meaningless if you are not dating someone. This is not at all true! You certainly need love and friendship – but these can be found in many different relationships. Dating can be a chance to know someone better, to spend more time with them, to share their life – to see if you are right for each other. But it can also make a relationship narrow and even selfish; it can bind your hearts in a way that might not be good for you now; and cut you off from other friendships. *So don't assume that you have to be dating all the time, or that there is something wrong with you if you are single.* If you are still young, or if you are not seriously considering marriage at this moment, then it is often better to stay single and put your time and emotional energy into strengthening friendships and getting to know new people. This gives your heart a kind of inner freedom to get stuck into other things; and it also means you have a bigger chance of meeting the right person when he or she comes along!

But don't put it off too long – There is a risk that people drift through their twenties, thinking about studies and qualifications and careers, and only begin to consider marriage seriously when they are well into their thirties. There are two drawbacks with this approach. First, it makes marriage seem like a 'second career', something that you do when you have done everything else you want to, something you enter into only when you have given the best of your time and energy to more demanding or worthwhile activities. Instead, *marriage, like every vocation, is something that you should want to give your best to.* This doesn't mean you have to marry young – the timing will depend on so many factors, not least on meeting the right person. But it does mean you should not put off the idea unnecessarily.

The other drawback with waiting too long is, putting it bluntly, that it gets harder to find someone. You shouldn't get in an unnecessary panic about this, and you can trust that God is guiding you whatever the circumstances of your lives. But it is often easier to meet different people when you are younger. People are more open to meeting others, more open to new friendships, less stuck in their ways. And it is more likely that a couple will be able to have children if they marry younger, without the struggles and anxieties of trying to conceive later on. *If you are older and looking for a husband or wife, do not lose hope. But if you are younger, then do be open to meeting others, and don't get so absorbed in your work and activities that marriage becomes an afterthought.*

The importance of friendship in dating – If you are dating, then of course you want to get to know the other person well and share your life with them. But a couple can get so involved with each other and their relationship and their feelings, that they never see the other person in a bigger context: with other people, with other friends, with their own family members. *You know someone partly through their relationships and their personal interests.* And if they have no other interests than you, then perhaps they are not very interesting! *Friendship is the most important part of dating: can you talk with each other, trust each other, forgive each other?* Do you have things in common? Can you share your joys and sorrows, your strengths and weaknesses, your dreams and fears? Do you like who they are and what they care about? Do you respect and admire their principles, the way they treat people? Can you share what is closest to your heart – your hopes, your values, your faith? Ultimately, if you are considering marriage, the deepest question is not just: do I love this person and do they love me? It is also: are they a good person, a person of faith, who would be kind and loving and faithful – as a husband and father, as a wife and mother?

Keep your relationship chaste while you are dating – *A chaste relationship when you are dating is one of the clearest signs that a marriage will be happy and faithful.* If you are having sex before marriage, or if you are getting sexually involved in a way that is too intimate before marriage, not only is this sinful, but it actually damages your relationship. It makes it harder for you to understand and trust each other as boyfriend and girlfriend. Dating, and then engagement, are about growing in love and friendship, so that you are ready to make the commitment of marriage. The paradox is that people are less ready for marriage if they are already sexually involved.

Living together, cohabitation, is not a good preparation for marriage, despite what many people think. It takes away your freedom to make a proper decision about the future, and it stops you being able to view the relationship in an objective way. It is no surprise that you are more likely to separate after marriage if you lived together before marriage. A couple is so involved, literally 'attached', that it becomes extra hard for them to see each other with clear eyes and a pure heart, and extra hard for them to step back and work out whether this is a truly good relationship. And if your boyfriend or girlfriend does not share your Catholic views about chastity before marriage, then he or she will probably not share your Catholic views about the true meaning of marriage itself.

There is much more to chastity than just abstinence. But *the decision not to have sex before marriage is a fundamental one that will bring you an inner peace*. It is a way of being faithful to your future husband or wife (because you are refusing to give your life in sexual love before marriage); it is a way of loving your present boyfriend or girlfriend and growing closer to them (because you are respecting the true nature of your relationship, which is one of friendship and affection); and it is a way of protecting your own purity of heart and freedom.

If you are still struggling to find a husband or wife – It is a source of great sadness and heartache to many people that they are finding it hard to meet someone. Perhaps you believe that marriage is the right vocation for you, and you have been looking for someone for a long time, and praying hard to find someone – but it hasn't happened yet. There are two pieces of advice here, and they may seem contradictory, but they are not. First, *don't lose hope*. Keep doing all the normal things that might help you to meet someone, keep praying (but don't become obsessive and pray too much), keep trying. Trust that God will lead you to someone if this is truly his plan for you. *Be patient and don't lose heart.* But at the same time, be at peace, and entrust your whole life and all your future to the Lord. Tell him that you accept his will in your life whatever that may be. Second, *don't cling to the idea of a future marriage in a way that makes it impossible for you to live and love in the present.* For any human being this kind of desperation can really damage our hearts. And for a Christian it can be a sign that we are clinging to our own plans and not trusting in the Lord and in his goodness. So you need to be hopeful and positive; but you also need to leave the results in God's hands let him do what is best. In a strange way it is necessary to hold onto the idea of marriage and to let go of it at the same time.

James, husband and father:
"I've always felt the pull of married life and always hoped I'd one day have some children to look after. Even at 17 years old I used to drift off and imagine being married with kids. I met Citra when I was in my early twenties when we both worked for the same Catholic newspaper – evidence of God's mysterious ways, as I was a non-Catholic at the time and didn't expect to meet my future wife, let alone contemplate, at length, the merits of Catholicism. A decade and four children later and I'm still as much in love with her as I was when I first clapped eyes on her. Of course, it's been extremely challenging, and without a strong faith I couldn't say

we'd be where we are now. If you build and feed a marriage on prayer and commitment the good times drown the bad and you learn to live and love whatever the circumstances."

Citra, wife and mother:

"I was always certain I would become a nun and often daydreamed about how I was going to change the world single-handedly. I prayed constantly about finding the right religious order to be exactly where I believed God wanted me. Marriage was definitely out. Then I met James. I tried to explain to him on many occasions that despite the fact that I liked him very much, I was definitely being called to higher things. But he wasn't put off and ten years and four beautiful children later, we are still very much in love. Furthermore, James converted to Catholicism some time ago and that ability we have to share our faith and apply it to our vocation has been a tremendous grace. It's true that 'man proposes and God disposes'. What God wanted for me really was what I had wanted all along, but hadn't discovered yet. Through prayer and an open heart, God always hears and answers, although, frustratingly, in his own time. Discerning our vocation often seems to be more a feat in patience and endurance than anything else. But perhaps that's the point. We need to get to that point of total surrender before he can work in our life. Then, no matter how far our will starts from God's will for us, the two will always finally meet."

10. What are the signs that God might be calling me to the priesthood or the consecrated life?

"Once you have renounced everything, really everything, then any bold enterprise becomes the simplest and most natural thing in all the world." (*Blessed Pope John XXIII*)

Consecrated life, as we saw in chapter 2, is the way of life embraced by those who dedicate themselves to the Lord by making lifelong vows of poverty, celibacy, and obedience that are recognised and accepted by the Church. This includes monks and nuns in enclosed monasteries and convents; religious brothers and sisters living in community who serve others through their apostolic work; and many other forms of consecrated life. The call to priesthood and the call to the consecrated life are different calls, so in one sense it is not fair to lump them together in this chapter. The life of a missionary sister, a Carthusian hermit, an enclosed nun, a parish priest, and a teaching friar are vastly different, and the particular pull towards each way of life will be very different. But the way God stirs up these vocations in our hearts can be quite similar. Here are some common signs and common ways of discerning a vocation to the priesthood or consecrated life. You don't need to tick every box here, but just pay attention to some of these areas and see if there are some recurring themes.

A desire to be a priest or consecrated person – Maybe you can't explain why you have this desire, *it's a part of you,* like falling in love. *You just know that this is what seems right.* You imagine yourself as a priest or consecrated person and it seems to fit, even if it makes you afraid or you think it would be impossible. *There is a joy and excitement when you think about it, a sense that this is the right path.* The idea keeps coming back – in your prayer, your daydreaming, your imagination. Some scripture passage or sermon seems to be directed at you – about the priesthood, or the call of the disciples, or service. These passages seem to stand out for you and have a kind of clarity; as if a light comes on; or it warms your heart; or it feels as if someone is pointing at you.

The desire may be long-term or gradual or recent – There are different kinds of desire. (i) *Some people have always wanted to be a priest or consecrated person:* they cannot remember a time when they did not have this desire; they pretended to be priests or consecrated persons when they were kids; it seems to be a part of them. (ii) *Some people have gradually wanted to be priests or consecrated persons:* it has grown over time; or it has come and gone; but now seems to be a bit stronger *and a bit more enduring. (iii) Some people have always wanted NOT to be a priest or consecrated person.* This might sound strange, but there are people who have always been fighting it, resisting, walking away, giving excuses why not; and this is because deep down they have always known it is a part of them; and at some point they realise that, in fact, people without vocations do not normally go around thinking about why they don't have a vocation! *(iv)* And *some people suddenly want to be priests or consecrated persons:* they have gone through a life changing spiritual experience; it has never occurred to them before but now it does; the priesthood or consecrated life is something new and sudden and unexpected, but very real and almost overpowering. This can happen, but these people need to be very cautious, because after a big adult conversion experience it is easy to confuse a desire to live a radical new Christian life (which is important for all people) with a desire to be a priest or consecrated person (which is only one way of responding to this new life, and perhaps not the right one). This is why the Church asks new converts to take time to settle into their new Catholic life for a few years before seeking ordination or consecrated life.

An admiration for priests or consecrated people you know – You sense a goodness and holiness in their lives. *You have an attraction to something they have or something they represent;* even if you can't imagine being one. *They seem to be living a life worth living, in a way that speaks to you. You are drawn to them.* Or perhaps you do not have any explicit desires to be a priest or consecrated person, but you are attracted to many of the things that are involved in their lives. You have a desire to serve people in different ways, or to pass on the faith, or to pray with and for others. Maybe you find less satisfaction in your work, not because it is wrong, but you feel it is not enough.

Sense of being pulled or pushed toward priesthood or consecrated life – This can be true even if you do not seem to have any real personal desire. In fact *it might seem like something you don't want to do, something you are fighting against.* The will of God and not your own will. It is *a nagging feeling that you should or could become a priest or consecrated person, that seems to come from nowhere, uninvited;* an idea you can't get out of your mind. It might leave you cold, or even repel you – in the sense that your instincts and gut fight against it. You may find yourself making excuses to yourself (and even to others) about why you shouldn't follow it, raising a list of objections, making clear all the signs that show you couldn't possibly do this. Perhaps you couldn't! But it is strange that you keep fighting and resisting it (when other people just don't bother thinking about it). It's as if part of you knows you should; there is an inner sense of duty, or call – even if it is reluctant.

An inner desire to pray more and to take the faith more seriously – You just find that you want to pray more and to deepen your faith. *Your love for Christ is growing, and your love for the Church. More and more you desire to give your life to God completely.* Of course this is true for many holy lay-people! But it can often be the beginning of a vocation to priesthood or consecrated life. You are not sure why, but you have a feeling that you can't hold anything back. *For some people the idea of celibacy comes to mean more and more* – not because they dislike marriage, but because they feel called to give their life wholeheartedly to serve God and others, in a way that would be difficult within the commitments of marriage and family life.

Other people affirm your vocation – When you talk to people about the possibility of priesthood or consecrated life, especially committed Catholics, they don't look as if you are mad. They affirm it, and say 'Of course, I could have told you that years ago'. *They encourage you.* In other words, from the outside, this vocation also seems to make sense – it is not just a subjective sign for you, but it is beginning to be a more objective sign to others too. *Perhaps people who don't know you even come up and suggest the priesthood or consecrated life to you,* out of the blue! The simple fact that someone unexpectedly suggests it to you, or jokes about it with you, may be the first sign of a call. They may see something you can't see, or something you are not prepared to admit that you see. You shouldn't assume that every person speaking to you is a messenger from God, and other people can sometimes get things wrong – but the suggestions others make might sometimes help you to reflect in a more open way.

Support from a wise person who knows you well – You may not have a formal 'spiritual director' (someone you speak to regularly about your faith), but perhaps there is someone wise and trustworthy that you have chatted to about your vocation over a period of time; you have talked things through with them and they know you quite well. *If they affirm what you have said,* and it seems to them that you may have a vocation, then this is another more public sign that it may be true. It could be a sign to take things further forward.

A feeling that you are not worthy to be a priest or consecrated person – This might seem like a paradox, but it can be true. Sometimes someone may have *a deep feeling that the priesthood or consecrated life is too much of an ideal for them, that they are not worthy, or not good enough,* or not capable enough. These feelings can be a sign of humility, an indication that someone has a healthy sense of their own limitations, and a high sense of the dignity of this calling. *The feeling of unworthiness may, strangely, be a sign that someone has a true appreciation for what this vocation means,* and that they will be open to asking for God's help and the help of the Church. It would be worrying if someone thought any kind of

Christian commitment was easy; or if they thought they could achieve it through their own efforts.

An attraction to marriage and family life – This might seem a strange point. Obviously, an attraction to marriage and family life is not a sign that you should become a priest or consecrated person. But it is true that *someone with a deep and strong pull towards marriage might be called by the Lord to become a priest or consecrated person.* God is not playing games and asking you to do what is impossible – to be married and not married at the same time. Rather, you may have a very natural desire for marriage and family, it's part of who you are as a man or woman, but the Lord might be calling you to let go of that so that you can discover another way of giving your life in love – as a priest or consecrated person. You need to look at all the other signs above; but this section is just to show you that an attraction to marriage does not necessarily mean you should rule out another vocation.

Women and the priesthood – The priesthood is a sacrament that can only be conferred on men. This is not just a Catholic rule that might be changed in a few years, it is Christ's own wish for the Church that has been confirmed by two thousand years of unbroken tradition. If you are a woman and you feel that there are strong signs of an attraction to the ministerial priesthood, these signs may indeed be God's way of calling you to a radical life of service and mission and responsibility, in the Church or in the world – but not as an ordained priest. *The Lord may be calling you to another vocation, that you can discover elsewhere in the Church, a place where you can live out your baptismal priesthood fully, and fulfil these deepest desires.* He may even be calling you to a form of life and service that has not been lived before in the Church, something new for our times, a role for you personally or for women more generally that is yet to be discovered. Be brave, be adventurous, don't lose heart. Be wise in your discerning. Follow the deepest calls in your heart, but be patient and humble too. Don't be tempted to give in to anger or despair. A vocation is always an inner movement of the heart that is confirmed by an outer confirmation from the Church. So if that confirmation is not there, then there will be another meaning to that inner call. Trust the Church when she says that the ministerial priesthood will not be an authentic answer to your call, and *pray that you will find another way of living this inner call fruitfully.*

Gerard, seminarian, preparing for Diocesan priesthood:
"One November evening I sensed God wanted me to consider becoming a priest. This call was a complete surprise to me. I had been working in the public sector for 20 years. I had not considered the priesthood. I responded because God was persistent. There was one thing I was certain about – the world needs God. People need to know and experience that there is a

God who loves them. People so often seem burdened. I used to struggle with how I might be able to help. How could I provide real assistance and not just lip service? I remember going to Mass and reflecting that the sacrifice of the Mass is being offered up at every hour of every day somewhere in the world. For Catholics that Mass is our nourishment, our lifeline. It was at this point that I realised the world needs the Eucharist and so the world needs priests. I was then able to say 'yes' to God's call. I am an ordinary man from an ordinary family. I do not have all the answers. But I am convinced that God exists and that he can provide the answers we all need. We have to be humble enough to seek his help."

Sr Clare, Poor Clare nun:

"My decision to become a nun was about falling in love with Jesus and wanting to give my life to him. This journey began through an encounter with a Franciscan Missionary sister I met at a 'Life in the Spirit' Seminar, and it took me five years to discern properly with my Spiritual Director before I was able to take the plunge and respond to the Lord's invitation to join Religious life. So what does being a Poor Clare mean for me? It means that God is fulfilling my deepest desires, for that which I desire most is also God's desire for me. When I say I am happy I am saying I feel fulfilled and alive in this life, it brings me true joy and peace at a deeper level. This is not a happiness without struggles, pain and constant challenges etc., but a deep felt happiness at the very centre of my being regardless of what life is throwing at me daily. Choosing to be a Poor Clare means I am able to give myself totally to Jesus in a way that I feel I cannot in any other vocation than as a nun."

11. How do I pursue a vocation to the priesthood or consecrated life?

Father, I abandon myself into your hands;
do with me what you will.
Whatever you may do, I thank you.
I am ready for all, I accept all.
Let only your will be done in me,
and in all your creatures;
I wish no more than this, O Lord.

Into your hands I commend my soul;
I offer it to you with all the love of my heart,
for I love you Lord,
and so need to give myself,
to surrender myself into your hands,
without reserve,
and with boundless confidence;
for you are my Father. (*Blessed Charles de Foucauld*)

Interpreting the signs – On their own, these signs listed in chapter 10 above are not a guarantee of a vocation to priesthood or consecrated life; they are different hints, small signs that the Lord may be speaking to you and calling you to priesthood or consecrated life. Like any language, they need interpreting, and you need help to interpret them. If it seems to you that some of these signs are very clear and strong, or if many of them seem to come together and add up and begin to form a pattern, then this can be the clearest sign that the Lord is calling you at least to investigate and humbly take the next step. And if these signs are missing, or they are very weak in your life, then the Lord is probably not calling you, at least not yet.

The overarching sign of a vocation will be *an enduring pull towards to the idea of priesthood or consecrated life, that is accompanied by a sense of peace and joy as you reflect on this attraction.* This does not mean the attraction will be without fears and anxieties and struggles (of course you are a bit anxious!). But if the idea of priesthood or consecrated life itself comes with a deep sense of panic or fear or anxiety (this is different from the natural humility and reluctance we feel) it may mean it is not right for you, and you would be much happier somewhere else! Usually, God gives us enough to go on – he does not play games with us.

Trying to move forward – There is no need to be paralysed or stuck. If you are discerning, that's fine. Follow the advice in chapter 5 about how to be open to your vocation. Be patient – things will become clearer. If you are really confused and stuck, and not sure which way to go, with contradicting signs and signals – then follow the advice in chapter 6, and try to make some kind of provisional decision.

Taking the next step – If these signs grow stronger and come together, then you should take the next step. It might be to talk to your parish priest, or the vocations director of the diocese, or the novice master or mistress of the congregation you are interested in. You move to a new stage in your discernment, which is trusting in the discernment of the Church. This discernment is more objective and 'public'. It involves other people, and ultimately it involves the Bishop or superior of the congregation. It can be difficult and humbling, because in some sense you are putting your future in the hands of others. *These are the people who have the final responsibility of calling people on behalf of Christ.* It is no longer just you trying to find what is right for yourself. If you eventually make an application to join, then you are trusting in the wisdom of those who assess your application. If you are accepted and begin formation, then you are trusting in the formation programme and the ongoing assessment process involved. All of these public responses are 'signs'; they are ways that the Lord helps you and guides you; and ultimately you should listen to them as much as to the personal signs of vocation you have discovered in your own life. *It is when your personal sense of calling comes together with the public response of the Church that you can be confident it is the right time to try and move forward.*

Trusting the Church – At the end of the day, *you can trust the Church to help you discern*. If the diocese or congregation encourages you and then formally accepts you, then this is a reasonable sign that the Lord is inviting you at least to take the next step into formation. It still leaves many years to discern and become sure – but you can have the assurance that you are doing the right thing for the moment. If the diocese or congregation holds you back or says no, then this is a reasonable sign that God is leading you to something else, something that is right for you, a different kind of vocation. Deep down, despite some possible disappointment, you can be grateful for the clarity this decision brings. And if the attraction doesn't go away, and other wise people encourage you, you can try again in different circumstances.

Certain essential requirements – There are certain basic requirements that you normally need if God is really calling you to the priesthood or consecrated life, and if these are lacking then this path is probably *not for you at this time in your life* – although it may show itself later on. This is just an informal explanation of some of these requirements – *you will need to talk to the vocations director or religious congregation to be clear about the official requirements*. It is really important to talk to someone about these areas (the vocations director; the novice master or mistress; your spiritual director). If something concerns you here, do not just panic and rule yourself out, as we often judge our situation too quickly or too harshly, and there may be other factors which are greatly in your favour.

The basic requirements that you need usually include: *A commitment to your Catholic faith* – a love for Christ, for the Sacraments, for the Church (even if you are aware of your weakness and failings). *A commitment to the commandments and to living a moral life* (even if you are weak and still struggle); you are trying to live a chaste life. *Basic physical and mental health* – serious medical conditions will make it difficult for you to live and work as a priest or consecrated person. *A personal and emotional maturity* – it will be very difficult for you to live in seminary or community, and to engage in pastoral work or a routine of prayer, if you have some deep and unresolved psychological issues; if you can't get on comfortably with different people; if you are really struggling with some kind of addiction or anything else that is dominating your life at this moment. *You are not married; you do not have any big responsibilities that would take away your freedom to become a priest or consecrated person* – e.g., children; huge debts; etc.

Which religious order or consecrated community? – A simple answer: *The one you are attracted to; the one you like; the one you feel at home in; the one whose ideals inspire you and whose members you admire*. All the normal signs of discernment listed above, all the ways that

God 'speaks' to you, are true for discovering the order or community that is right for you. If you feel a calling to consecrated life but have not found the right place, then make sure you have a good look at what is out there. Read about the different forms of consecrated life. Read the lives of the saints to discover which kinds of life inspire you. Talk to a wise priest or consecrated person who can advise you about which orders or communities might suit you. And when your interest is stirred up, *go and visit some – sharing their life, talking to the members*. You don't have to visit every order or community to make a decision, but you have to make an effort and look into things. Trust that through your 'research' and prayer God will guide you to the right place.

Fr Anthony, priest, Canon Regular of the Lateran:
"I grew up in a time when a vocation to the priesthood was greatly esteemed and held in awe. It was something people prayed for. It was part of the Catholic ethos. It manifested itself in people's attitude to the Mass and reverence for priests. My earliest memory is of standing with my parents at the top of the road waiting for a lift to Mass. We lived in a remote part of Cornwall and depended on the goodness of priests to help us. Every effort had to be made to get to Mass, even in war time, and even though the Mass station was several miles away. The care of the priest was appreciated and his visit to the home welcomed. In London they came round after an air-raid. In the country they did everything to provide Mass in

remote centres and tried to see that the children received instruction. And so when the priest on visiting our house remarked to my mother, 'That boy should be a priest', that was all I needed to get things going."

Przemek, considering a vocation to a Benedictine monastery:

"I have been struggling to reconcile my faith with everyday life in some meaningful and personal way pretty much my entire adult life, and I am twenty-nine now. Intuitions about becoming a religious were a big part of that struggle, but I had always thought that I either was not good enough or that this was my mind trying to escape from 'reality'. So I continued with my 'double life'. In 2004 I came to England to study. The chaplain at my university suggested I go on a retreat in Pluscarden Abbey. I went there in the summer of 2005 and quickly found out that life of a monk is not an escape from life, anything but, in fact. Surprisingly, this "discovery" only increased my longing for religious life, but it took me another two years to consciously admit that and prepare myself to take things forward. Then I went through a phase of enthusiasm for every possible form of religious life, thankfully that's gone too. What is left is this initial attraction and longing that has always been with me, and which increased when I visited Pluscarden Abbey and whenever we joined the Worth community for prayer. In other words, I think that God calls me to be a monk. I may still be wrong, but I am at peace with that possibility too. After all, the desire to please God does in fact please him, as Thomas Merton put it, probably paraphrasing my favourite Saint Augustine."

12. What are the signs that God might be calling me to the Permanent Diaconate?

"God has created me to do him some definite service; he has committed some work to me which he has not committed to another. I have my mission – I may never know it in this life, but I shall be told it in the next. I am a link in a chain, a bond of connection between persons.

He has not created me for naught. I shall do good, I shall do his work; I shall be a preacher of truth in my own place, while not intending it, if I do but keep his commandments and serve him in my calling.

Therefore, my God, I will put myself without reserve into your hands. What have I in heaven, and apart from you, what do I want upon earth? My flesh and my heart fail, but God is the God of my heart, and my portion forever." (*Cardinal John Henry Newman*)

The permanent diaconate is open to both single and married men. *If a married man is thinking about the permanent diaconate it is essential that he discerns this vocation with his wife, so that it is a decision made within the unity of one's marriage.* For the married man ordination to the diaconate is meant to grow out of and complement his marriage. These are just some signs that God might be calling you to the permanent diaconate, some of the ways that God might be guiding you in your life. It is the overall pattern that is important. The paragraphs about marriage obviously apply only to those who are married. If you are interested in finding out more about the permanent diaconate then talk to your parish priest or get in touch with the Director for Permanent Deacons in your home diocese.

A stable and supportive marriage – No marriage is perfect, but you and your wife must have a solid and supportive relationship. There are no major issues in your marriage that make it hard for you to communicate with each other or live your Catholic faith with integrity. *You are able to make this decision about ordination together in a mature way.* You both believe that the commitment to the diaconate, in the time of formation and in the ministry itself, *will not be an unnecessary burden for your marriage and family, but rather an enrichment.*

A commitment to your Catholic faith and to your prayer life – *You love your faith and it has been an important part of your life for a long time.* You treasure it for yourself, you have made time to grow in your understanding of the faith, and you long to share it with others. You try to pray within the circumstances of your working life. You value prayer. You appreciate in a personal way the importance of the sacraments, especially of the Mass.

A commitment to family and work – *You love and care for your wife and family,* despite the inevitable struggles. You are faithful to your responsibilities at work and you are able to give generously of your time and yourself whenever there is need.

A desire to serve – You have already shown a commitment to serve others in different ways, in the parish or in other voluntary situations. You have the time and energy and proven capacity to work for others and to work willingly. *You have a desire to serve others more wholeheartedly, as a vocation. You are drawn especially to the service you see in the lives of deacons:* assisting at the altar in the sacramental celebrations, preaching and teaching God's Word, leading people in prayer, and serving others in the ministry of charity. This will extend especially to the poor and the marginalised; and one of your particular responsibilities as a deacon will be to bring their needs to the notice of your parish and the wider church.

Human qualities – You have all the human qualities that will allow you to be a worthy minister in God's Church. *You have the emotional and psychological maturity to take on a new and demanding role.* You are able to take the lead, and you have experience in different leadership roles. You can work well with others and win their respect.

The encouragement of others – *Other people in the parish encourage you to think about the diaconate,* or support you when you discuss the idea. They can see you in this ministry; they can imagine that you would do it well and that you would find happiness in it.

The encouragement of your parish priest – *A key person in your discernment and in supporting you will be your parish priest.* If he believes that you are being called to the permanent diaconate, and if he supports you in your application, then this is a very positive sign.

The place of celibacy – *A single man commits himself to lifelong celibacy* from the moment of his ordination as a permanent deacon. A married man does not – he continues to live the fullness of his marriage, but he *makes a promise that if his wife dies before him he will remain celibate and will not remarry.* This is a very serious commitment, especially if there are young children in the family and there is an anxiety about how they might be brought up or cared for should their mother die.

Rev James, husband, father, and grandfather; permanent deacon:

"It started when my parish priest said to me: "Is there any reason why I should not put your name forward for consideration to become a permanent deacon?" My reaction was one of total confusion and I walked home to think more and to discuss everything with Diane, my wife. A few days later and with a mixture of confusion with a determination to see this to some sort of conclusion, I returned to my parish priest and said I was willing to go through the selection process. Four years later I was ordained and in the process experienced something as life-changing as marriage and becoming a father. Those two life events are also vocations with the diaconate joining them and the Church firmly stating that my vocation of marriage must not suffer because of my ordination. As someone who was baptised and entered the Church aged 39 it was not, in itself, strange to experience yet another radical step in my faith journey."

Rev Charlie, husband and father; permanent deacon:
"I first thought of becoming a permanent deacon when I was on a retreat about five years ago. It was like a whisper in my heart - sometimes there, sometimes not. I had always thought that the diaconate was for older, retired men; however, my brother encouraged me to respond and suggested that I get in touch with the diocesan vocations director. I did this and before very long I started the four year process of formation and preparation. It was during this time that gradually I became more sure that the Lord was leading me on this path – my studies went well, the formation staff were happy with my progress, and my wife was supportive, in fact we used to go to the study days together. Gradually the whisper became more of a certainty; and for me, a week's retreat in Assisi about a month before my ordination was most significant – there I experienced a sense of completeness. I was ordained in May 2008 – it was a most memorable day, full of grace."

Conclusion

"Make sure that you let God's grace work in your souls by accepting whatever he gives you, and giving him whatever he takes from you. True holiness consists in doing God's will with a smile. Give yourself fully to God. He will use you to accomplish great things on the condition that you believe much more in his love than in your own weakness." (*Mother Teresa of Calcutta*)

As you discern your vocation and think about God's plan for your life: be at peace! Or as Padre Pio often used to say: "*Pray, hope, and don't worry!*". The Lord loves you and cares for you. He is guiding you along every step of your journey. Do all you can to live your faith with integrity and joy. *Do all you can to discern your vocation. Do all you can to follow God's will, as far as you know it. And leave the rest to him, he won't let you down!*

Put everything, especially your vocation, into the hands of the Blessed Virgin Mary. She is a spiritual mother to every Christian. She cares for you personally; she prays for you by name; and she longs to see you happy and fulfilled in your Christian life. All the gifts and guidance that God the Father gives you, all the graces of the Holy Spirit, come through the intercession of Jesus Christ our High Priest, and through the prayers of the Blessed Virgin. So entrust your concerns about your vocation to her, and make a point of saying a prayer to her every day for help and guidance. If you are not sure what prayer to say, simply pray the Hail Mary each evening for this intention. She never leaves anyone forsaken.

Mary, wife and mother:
"My soul glorifies the Lord, my spirit rejoices in God, my Saviour. He looks on his servant in her lowliness; henceforth all ages will call me blessed. The Almighty works marvels for me. Holy his name! His mercy is from age to age, on those who fear him. He puts forth his arm in strength and scatters the proud-hearted. He casts the mighty from their thrones and raises the lowly. He fills the starving with good things, sends the rich away empty. He protects Israel, his servant, remembering his mercy, the mercy promised to our fathers, to Abraham and his sons for ever."

Further information

The different vocations – The National Office for Vocation has some information and links concerning all the vocations: http://www.ukvocation.org/ See especially the section 'Callings'. **Discerning** – There are many groups in the Church set up to help people discern their vocation. One such is Compass, which has an excellent website: http://www.compass-points.org.uk with prayers and links to various religious orders. **Marriage** – If as a couple you are thinking of getting married, the first port of call for advice and marriage preparation will always be your parish priest. **Priesthood** – An official website for Diocesan Priesthood is: http://www.ukpriest.org/ If you are considering the Diocesan priesthood, then contact the Vocations Director in your home diocese. If you are not sure of his details, ask your parish priest, or search online for your diocesan website. **Consecrated life** – If you are considering consecrated life, then do get in touch with any congregations or associations you have heard of or been attracted to. If you don't know where to start, there are links to the websites of various congregations at: http://www.corew.org/members.htm. The National Conference of Secular Institutes also has a website: http://www.secularinstitutes.co.uk/. **Permanent Diaconate** – If you are considering the Permanent Diaconate, then talk to your parish priest, or contact the

Director for Permanent Deacons in your diocese. If you are not sure of his details, ask your parish priest, or search online for your diocesan website. **Living your faith** – The booklet *A Way of Life for Young Catholics,* by Fr Stephen Wang (also published by the Catholic Truth Society) is full of practical advice about how to live your Catholic faith and be more open to the Lord. It also lists many good books and websites about the Catholic faith, and suggests various communities and movements within the Church that might help you in your journey of faith.

RADICAL DISCIPLESHIP
Consecrated Life and
the Call to Holiness

FRANCIS CARDINAL ARINZE

This work illuminates the vocation of the consecrated state and its presence in the Body of Christ, beginning with a brief look at its origins in Scripture and the early Church. It reflects on the different forms this radical life takes, the population of consecrated persons in the Church today, the recognition that the consecrated life has received from the Church, the vows of Poverty, Chastity and Obedience taken by all consecrated persons, and more.

RADDISC-P... 112 pp., Paperback, $11.95

(IHS) ignatius press

ignatius.com • (800) 651-1531

LIFEWORK
Finding Your Purpose in Life

DR. RICK SARKISIAN

This unique approach to discovering the presence of God in all that we do emphasizes the personal vocation and mission to which we are called. Written in a user-friendly style, this book is particularly relevant for high school, college and young adult age groups, yet applies to all believers wanting to seek God's will and purpose. You will develop an awareness of your individual talents, gifts, abilities, occupational preferences, and educational options. For the first time, vocation, mission, and lifework choices are offered in one book.

LFYP-P... 135 pp., Paperback, $14.95

ignatius press

ignatius.com • (800) 651-1531

LIVE A LIFE
SHAPED BY MERCY

7 SECRETS OF DIVINE MERCY
VINNY FLYNN

In this compelling and timely book and talk, best-selling author and speaker Vinny Flynn draws from Scripture, the teachings of the Church, and the Diary of St. Faustina to reveal the heart of Divine Mercy. He offers an invitation and a road map so that Divine Mercy, the overflow of love from the Holy Trinity, can transform your life.

AVAILABLE AS A BOOK AND AS AN AUDIO PRESENTATION

 Call **(866) 767-3155** to order
or visit **LighthouseCatholicMedia.org**

INSPIRING TALKS
THAT CHANGE LIVES

BELOVED
Dr. Tim Gray

Dr. Gray presents Biblical principles for finding happiness in marriage, and the blessings and struggles of married life.

EVANGELIZING CATHOLICS
Dr. Scott Hahn

Dr. Hahn discusses why evangelization is the Church's greatest priority, and how we are all called to share our faith.

MADE FOR GREATNESS
Leah Darrow

Leah shares how the pursuit of pop culture's definition of happiness led her to a moment of mercy and conversion.

OVER 300 CDs, BOOKS, BOOKLETS, & PAMPHLETS AVAILABLE

LIGHTHOUSE CATHOLIC MEDIA

Call **(866) 767-3155** to order
or visit **LighthouseCatholicMedia.org**

Download the free
CATHOLIC STUDY BIBLE APP
IGNATIUS-LIGHTHOUSE EDITION

A free digital version of the entire Bible (RSV-2CE)

- Ignatius Study Bible notes and commentary available for purchase
- Dramatized audio New Testament* available for purchase
  (**FREE** audio of the Gospel of John)
- 10 hours of **FREE** audio commentary from Dr. Scott Hahn
- Over 200 Lighthouse talks available for purchase

* Includes a foreword from Pope Emeritus Benedict XVI

AVAILABLE FOR:

 iPad iPhone
iPod touch   Google play   kindle fire

Search **CATHOLIC STUDY BIBLE** in the App Store

INTRODUCT

Explains the Chak

existing at different levels of

human system, both from the traditional Eastern
viewpoint and within the framework of Western
mystery teaching exemplified by the Qabalah. For
all students of the occult who seek the expansion of
human consciousness.

3.50

INTRODUCTION
TO THE
CHAKRAS

by

PETER RENDEL

THE AQUARIAN PRESS
Wellingborough, Northamptonshire

First published 1974
Second Edition, completely
revised, enlarged and reset 1979

© PETER RENDEL 1979

6   8   10   9   7

*All rights reserved. No part of this book may be reproduced or utilized in any
form or by any means, electronic or mechanical, including photocopying,
recording or by any information storage and retrieval system, without permission
in writing from the Publisher.*

ISBN 0 85030 161 0

The Aquarian Press is part of the Thorsons Publishing Group

Printed and bound in Great Britain by
Richard Clay (The Chaucer Press) Ltd.,
Bungay, Suffolk

CONTENTS

The veil of Isis sevenfold
To him as gauze shall be,
Wherethrough, clear-eyed, he shall behold
The Ancient Mystery.

INTRODUCTION

This book is written for the student who has already done a certain amount of yoga and meditation practice and wants to move forward into a deeper understanding of the principles which underlie this fascinating and rewarding subject. We feel that in view of the explosion in popularity of the subject of yoga in recent years many people will shortly, if they do not already, fall into this category.

The aim of yoga is the expansion of human consciousness so that it is eventually identified with universal consciousness. This is to be achieved by a realization of the ultimate spiritual principle within ourselves; that which is above the physical and mental and is in fact our own true Eternal Self.

To achieve this one must learn to recognize these different principles or levels within oneself; in other words learn to distinguish the finer from the grosser. Therefore one must learn to work with and control the energies in oneself. Eventually one comes to realize that all Life, including oneself, is just energy in different states or in different rates of vibration. These energies in one's own system are what the chakras are all about. The chakras are the vital force centres at the different levels of experience or consciousness in the human system.

The word *chakra* means a wheel in Sanskrit and these centres of energy may be seen as wheels or vortices of force. The energies seated at these levels manifest through these vital force centres.

This book is intended for the essentially practical student who is prepared to discover deeper realities within himself. An academic or mental understanding of a thing is not the same as actually experiencing it although it may precede that experience. No one else can know something for you any more than he can eat your food for you. These realizations can therefore only be attained by one's own efforts.

The man who sets out to discover these truths must be a spiritual adventurer. He must have the attitude of the explorer: the urge to discover new worlds and new dimensions within; the desire to explore inner space; the perseverance to succeed in his quest.

This book presents the subject not only from the traditional Eastern viewpoint but also attempts to reconcile with it the Western mystery teaching which comes down to us through such traditions as the Qabalah, hermeticism, alchemy and astrology. It is not always easy to see the whole pattern of a subject underlying its many different facets and presentations but we hope the pattern may be somewhat clarified in this presentation of the subject.

Chapters One to Six explain the occult anatomy of man. Here the structure of man's system is outlined and the magnetic polarities and energy fields are explained as they relate to the flow of vitality and the seven chakras of his system. These are the very essence of his whole being.

Chapters Seven to Nine deal with the application of these principles in practice through yoga and self training. However, these principles need not necessarily only be termed yoga. Throughout the centuries mystics and seekers have followed these same principles under numerous other names and whatever name suits an individual best is the right one for him providing it embodies the true principles.

Finally, Chapter Ten traces the relationship between astrology and the chakras. Some ideas concerning the zodiac and the planets are also considered in relation to them.

In this field of study the *modus operandi* should be:

        (*a*) Recognizing
        (*b*) Controlling
        (*c*) Using

(*a*) To learn to recognize the principles involved and the energies which constitute the system.

(*b*) To learn to use these energies within oneself.

(*c*) To learn to use these energies creatively and unselfishly in Life.

We feel that the reader who follows these rules will gain a greater insight into life and will be richly rewarded by a deeper knowledge of himself.

CHAPTER ONE

THE BASIC POLARITY

In order to understand the chakras or vital force centres and how they relate to each other and to the whole of one's being, one must first begin by studying how the essential polarities of Spirit and Matter come into existence.

The Trinity

Any manifestation that takes place must result in a polarity or duality; if such a polarity does not occur then there can be no manifestation. The relationship between these two poles is the third aspect of the Trinity.

To prove this point, let us take any simple action as an example and see how the principle applies. Suppose the reader now says to himself 'I will close this book', in doing this he manifests an activity and thus brings into being a polarity of subject and object. The subject is 'I', the object 'the book', and the relationship between them 'will close' is the verb. If the reader should consider that this is merely playing with words let him try to think of any action that does not fall into these three parts and he will find that this is impossible.

Thus in the manifesting of any activity this threefold division is inevitably and inescapably produced and nothing can actually happen or take place in the world of name and form which does not take this triple form. This is the Trinity which is fundamental to so many religions and metaphysical systems and philosophies of the world, such as the Christian Trinity and the three gunas of Hinduism.

Names for this polarity are numerous, and we are accustomed to such terms as: Life and Form; Spirit and Matter; Perceiver and Perceived; Self and Not Self. We also use the terms Unity and Diversity because the subject or perceiver is always one whereas the objective or perceived side of life is always diverse. This is often represented by the symbol of the wheel.

If we consider the subject, verb and object aspects of the Trinity to be 'I am that', then the 'I' or perceiver at the centre of the wheel is one, but as manifestation occurs and life moves out from that central point into its objective form, diversity must inevitably come about. Thus at the rim of the wheel the spokes must be separate but at the centre they must be one. Therefore in its objective form, life will involve relationship and separation and all that goes with this: such as cause and effect, time and the law of becoming, birth, death and rebirth. This is the objective aspect of 'I am that'; whereas at the subjective level there is only the consciousness of pure 'I am' with no objective side. Therefore there is no experience of change, time, separation, relationship and those aspects of the objective side of life.

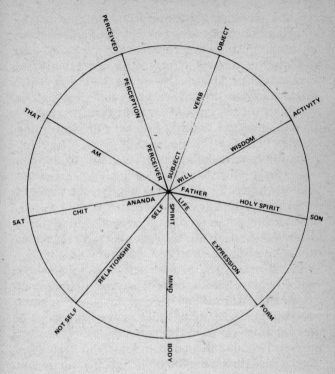

It is not difficult to think of numerous other terms used for this essential polarity such as Good and Evil or God and Devil, depending upon the religious or metaphysical system concerned. There can be no complete system of metaphysics or science of life which does not include this polarity. The Chinese terminology for these polarities has an especial merit as the words Yin and Yang express through their actual sounds the principles they define. Yin is essentially a subjective sound whereas Yang is an objective one. These sounds are reflected in the English words 'spirit' and 'matter' also involving the narrow or subjective *i* and the broad or objective *a*. Also in the words 'this' and 'that' which likewise express subject and object. The words 'thin' and 'fat' have similar characteristics – the fine subjective *i* having a higher rate of vibration than the broad objective *a*.

Naturally any experience in order to have a significance must have two poles or possibilities between which it can occur; therefore the whole of life is really the varied experiences resulting from the interplay or relationship between these poles. One may illustrate this by a simple example such as that of a game or sport played by two players or teams. If one of the two parties always won there would be no significance or worthwhile experience gained from it; or if one party always lost the same would apply. The significance of the experience of playing it derives from the open possibility of either losing or winning the game. Similarly in life, all the experience through which we grow and evolve derives from our being placed within this polarity of Spirit and Matter, Yin and Yang, Self and Not Self and the way in which this relationship plays through our consciousness. These polarities, the subjective and objective sides of our being and their combinations, permutations and intermediate stages constitute our total experience and is sometimes called the 'Dance of Yin and Yang'. We shall refer to this in more detail in later chapters.

Eastern Religions

Life, therefore, is both an upward and a downward process: flowing out from its source into manifestation and returning to its source with an added experience gained from that descent. In Christian terms, the soul returns with its harvest of experience 'Bearing its sheaves with it'. Traditional Eastern religions such as Buddhism and Hinduism are principally concerned with what one may term the withdrawal aspect of life through detachment of the spiritual principle from its involvement in the form of material aspect. These religions are mainly laying emphasis on the joy and bliss which is experienced when the soul is able to withdraw from its attachment to the personal self and achieve union with the higher spiritual principle within. The word 'personal' derives from the Latin *persona* meaning a mask and its use therefore indicates the transient or unreal nature of the lower self as being something which we put on at birth through which to express ourselves but which is not our real Self.

This union with the divine principle within us, our higher or real Self, is termed yoga in Hindu metaphysics. The word 'yoga', in fact, means union. It comes down to us in the English word 'yoke'. The Latin word *yugum* is derived from it and gives us the English word 'conjugal'.

In the Muslim religion the concept of union is expressed through the term *Islam*, meaning surrender of the lower self to the higher divine principle in oneself. Self-surrender is an essential of all mysticism, and Christianity has expressed this concept as Communion or the Mystical Marriage.

Other philosophies, particularly Western ones, are more concerned with the aspect of bringing down the spiritual principle and expressing it in form through creative activity.

Neither of these is wholly right, or rather, each expresses a partial truth and so each is right only within its own limitation and both are necessary parts of the whole process of Life. Life is therefore both descent from one's source and return to it, and ideally one should balance the two processes. These two aspects may be termed magical and mystical, the path of descent being magic and the path of return mysticism.

Phases of Life

Most of us will not find it difficult to recognize types of people, either living or historical, who strongly embody one or the other of these aspects. Great spiritual teachers, yogis and saints are those on the mystical path whereas those such as social reformers and great inventors are mainly on the magical path, expressing spirit through form. We recognize too in ourselves these principles in our moods or states of consciousness which predominate at different times. At certain times we may seek solitude in deep meditation or communion with nature while at others we may feel the urge to express ourselves through creative activity at the material level, or by communication with others. Of course at the spiritual level no otherness exists so that the principle of communication no longer applies because one is experiencing oneness with *all* Life.

Our experience is a vibration between the two poles of Aloneness when at the spiritual level and Togetherness when communicating at the personal level in a group or partnership. Aloneness derives from All-one-ness which is the experience of wholeness or integration at the spiritual level.

These phases of life may correspond to age, sex and other factors, which are continually changing in emphasis according to the flow of life's becomingness. The rhythms or cycles which occur as the life force relates between Yin and Yang are of great importance to the serious student who seeks to know himself. They are sometimes referred to as the Tattwic Tides. Further reference to this will be made in a later chapter.

Men and women on the whole find it difficult to balance their lives and find the right relationship at any one time between the polarities in themselves. Life does not stand still but is a continuous flow or vibration between the poles. Therefore every moment of time brings a new relationship – a new experience and a new activity needed on the part of each person to fully live that experience.

Arthur Koestler expressed this as an apparent conflict between the principles in his essay 'The Yogi and the Commisar' as typifying spiritual and material man. Most people tend to remain at one level only; to be able to move between the two poles at will requires skill and discipline. They finally learn that the two principles are not adversaries but in reality are the closest of allies and they are able to balance, keeping their heads in the clouds and their feet on the ground, continually drawing on spirit and expressing it through form.

When one principle is pursued too strongly there is always the tendency for the energy to swing back to the other in order to balance. This explains the sudden changes which seem to occur in people's lives. For example, men and women who are disappointed in physical love often find the energies reacting from the lower levels and swinging upwards so that they become intensely spiritual, for a time at any rate. And on the other hand, men and women who push themselves too hard towards the

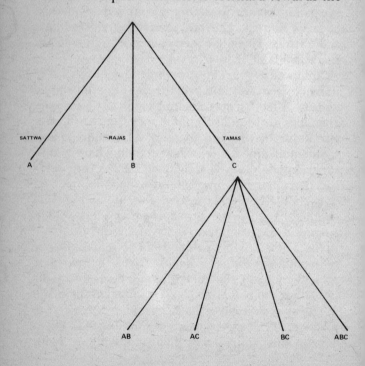

spiritual plane often react by having the energies swing down into strong physical and material desires. The old saying 'The greater the sinner the greater the saint' or vice versa is equally true whichever way round it is expressed.

Now let us try to take these principles a stage further and see how numerologically this trinity or triplicity gives rise to the numbers 4 and 7.

From the essential or primordial unity we have seen how three must always arise in manifestation and from this triplicity a lower quaternary is born. This is so because three principles can only group themselves in four further combinations in which none of the original three is repeated. Thus if we have A, B and C these can only combine as AB, AC, BC and ABC.

The higher triplicity, 3, and the lower quaternary, 4, make 7. It is thus that mathematically and by a further stage of densification spirit descends into form and the number 7 is manifested, bringing the important sevenfold divisions in colour and sound and giving us the seven levels of consciousness in man (that is the seven chakras) with which we are now concerned.

CHAPTER TWO

THE SEVEN PRINCIPLES IN MAN

We shall now trace the way in which the sevenfold division already described in the previous chapter relates to Man. We shall see how it produces the seven levels of his consciousness and his seven centres of vital force – the chakras.

In man the essential polarity which we have discussed in Chapter One has its axis along the spinal column so that spirit has its manifestation at the crown of the head while matter (in its densest form) manifests at the root of the spine. Between these poles there are intermediate stages of consciousness, each denser than the preceding one as the life force descends down the spine in its involution into matter. One may compare this process of gradual densification with the vibratory effects which are produced in music from the string of an instrument. The deeper notes are produced as the result of the string vibrating more slowly; when the string of the instrument vibrates more quickly it produces a higher note. So it is also that the finer levels of our consciousness are the Life Force vibrating at a higher frequency and the lower frequencies are the grosser or more material levels within ourselves.

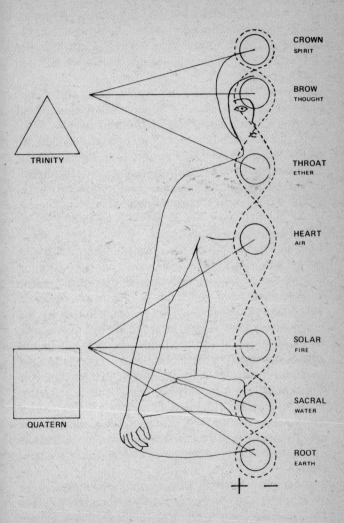

TRINITY

QUATERN

CROWN
SPIRIT

BROW
THOUGHT

THROAT
ETHER

HEART
AIR

SOLAR
FIRE

SACRAL
WATER

ROOT
EARTH

+ −

The seven chakras in man therefore correspond to a seven-note musical scale, the lower chakras having a slower vibration and corresponding to the deeper notes of the scale and the higher chakras to the finer notes.

St Paul defined Man as 'Spirit, Soul and Body' and one can readily see that this definition is based upon the three principles of the Trinity which we have discussed in Chapter One. Spirit and body are the basic polarities and *thought* is the relationship between the two. St Paul was using the Greek word *psyche* implying the mental and emotional level which we will now term *mind* instead of Soul.

The Elements
Let us see how this definition fits in with the chakras in Man.

Spirit we have already noted manifests at the crown of the head and the next chakra to appear in order of density is the force centre between the eyebrows, which St Paul refers to as soul (but which we may now call mind) being the seat of mental activity. Next in order is the throat centre and this, as St Paul said, is the body in essence because it is the seat of the ether. The ether is the substratum from which the four lower elements, air, fire, water and earth, are derived. Each of these elements is merely a modification of the basic ether so that the ether may rightly be regarded as the basic material body.

The four elements of air, fire, water and earth have their seats respectively at the heart, solar plexus, sacral and root chakras. In this way we see that the higher triplicity and lower quaternary appear in Man strictly in accordance with the numerical laws of manifestation and the seven chakras are an exact working out of these laws.

Alchemists referred to the ether as the quintessence or fifth level of vibration and we shall see later how the four lower elements are both produced from and return to this etheric substratum or latency. The more advanced alchemists also realized that since the various levels of consciousness are merely the life force vibrating at different frequencies, it follows that one level may be transmuted into another merely by changing the rate of vibration, and hence the transformation of one element into another is a perfectly natural possibility. This also applies to the transmutation of our grosser vibrations into our finer ones. The esoteric alchemy dealt with the refinement of man's consciousness by purification until the dross of the lower self was entirely transmuted and the pure gold of spiritual consciousness was attained. This process of attainment is known under various names to all true mystics of whatever religion.

In more modern times Einstein and other well-known physicists have noted the fact that matter is thought, vibrating at a lower frequency. In earlier times alchemists performed their transmutations of one metal into another using the same principles. In fact all manifestation is merely the life force working at different rates of vibration and the difference between one element and another is merely its different frequency of vibration.

The Sequence of Involution

The body, as we have seen, is really the third or objective aspect of the trinity – that is the ether. Its four modifications comprise, air, fire, water and earth. The sequence of involution may be expressed in the following way:

For an objective manifestation to occur there must first be space within which it can do so. Therefore ether is the element of pure space alone.

Next there must be locomotion within that space and this is the element of air which is motion alone within that space.

Next there must come into being the principle of expansion which is the element of fire.

This is followed by the principle of contraction which is the element of water.

Finally the principle of solidity or cohesiveness manifests which is the element of earth.

These principles or elements are often referred to by the Sanskrit term *tattwas* meaning 'thatness' or 'suchness'. This means the essence of any quality. These elements are all that there is, in fact there is nothing else except them in the world of name or form. They are the bricks of which our total experience is built and the world of manifestation is composed solely of the elements.

CHAPTER THREE

THE FOUR POLE MAGNET

We have outlined the way in which the vertical polarity of man comes into being along the axis of the spine with its seven levels of consciousness.

In addition to this vertical polarity, man's constitution also provides a horizontal polarity. This gives a positive and negative polarity to the two sides of his body. Thus man is really a quadripolar magnet and all the laws of electricity and magnetism which are known to modern physics apply to his system.

In any system, a potential difference between two poles gives rise to a flow between them. In electrical terms this potential difference is a voltage and the amount of flow between the poles can be measured as current. Where there is a flow of current there is always a magnetic field surrounding it and at right angles to it. This law also applies to the system in Man: in Man there is a voltage and current between his basic polarity of crown and root. This flow gives rise to a magnetic field which surrounds him. This magnetic field is what is very often termed the aura and is visible to those who have a sufficiently sensitive and delicate sense of sight.

Thus in man's occult anatomy there are two currents of energy which flow on the right and left sides and which are positive and negative. These positive and negative currents of energy seem to cross at nodes or points between the chakras. In this way the pattern of the Caduceus or Staff of Hermes is built up. In Hindu terminology this is called the *Meru Danda*.

The Caduceus

There are several interesting features concerning this pattern of forces which we will now discuss:

Each chakra is a vortex of energy which revolves under the influence of a positive and negative current acting upon it in just the same way as the rotor of an electric motor revolves when positive and negative electric currents are applied to it.

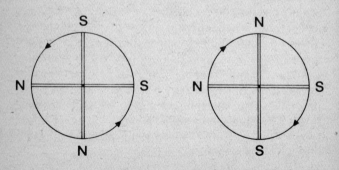

When the polarity of the current is reversed so that the positive and negative currents are each changed to the opposite pole, the electric motor will of course change the direction of its revolution.

An identical process takes place at each chakra.

The current flowing on one side of the body is positive and on the other is negative. As these currents cross at the nodes the positive one being dominant causes the chakra to revolve in its own direction. In effect, therefore, each chakra appears to revolve in the opposite direction to the one above and below it.

These points lead to a further conclusion based upon the laws of electricity known to modern science. A conductor placed within an electric coil through which current is flowing will conduct a current along its length in one direction. When the flow is reversed in the coil so also is the flow reversed in the conductor.

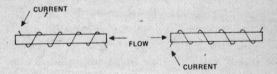

Likewise, the energy at the hub of the chakra will be outgoing or incoming according to the direction in which it is revolving. The direction of its revolution is itself determined by the influence of the positive and negative currents through the right and left sides of the body.

Alternating Currents
However, these currents are not direct but are
alternating ones. Here again the alternation of the
currents is a similar process to that occurring when
electricity is generated. As the rotor of the dynamo
revolves between the poles of the fixed magnet it
cuts the lines of force first in one direction and then
in the other so that a current is produced which
alternates in its direction of flow. This is the
alternating current which we use in our present-day
electric power system.

This process also relates to the flow of energy
round the surface of the earth due to the diurnal
rotation of the earth on its axis.

As the earth revolves between midday and
midnight the current flows towards the sun, but
during the other half of its revolution between
midnight and midday the current (also sweeping
towards the sun) will flow in the opposite direction.

Man is a microcosm of the macrocosm and this
process is similarly reflected in his system.
Therefore his energy currents also alternate
between his polarities – north-south, east-west.

These energy currents are in fact the breath. This
is the reason why the breath is of vital importance,
and we deal with this in greater detail later in the

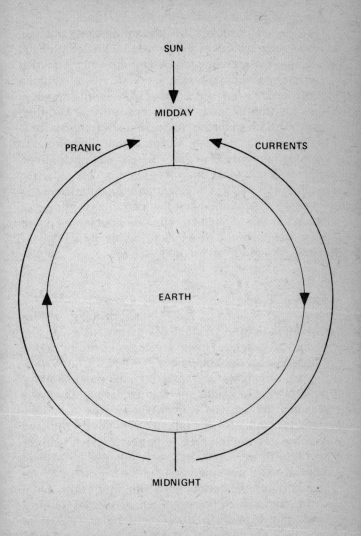

book. At various times the breath predominates through one nostril or the other. The alternation of the breath in this way produces the change of direction in the flow of energy currents and the revolution of the chakras.

We have seen that each level of consciousness is a basic vibration and these vibrations are called *tattwas* in Hindu terminology. In western terms they may be called elements, temperaments or humours. As the currents flow in various ways, different tattwas or elements manifest more or less strongly in the system. Our systems, therefore, are subject to continuous change and a continuous flow of humours as one element runs its course and gives place to another. The whole principle of this flow of changing vibrations is often known as the *Tattwic Tides*.

Tattwic Tides

The flow of tattwic tides in the human system corresponds to the flow of tattwic tides in the universal system. This is the basis of the hermetic adage 'As above so below'. The flow of tattwas in the universal system manifests as the planetary influences, the signs of the zodiac and as the seasons. Within the human system too there are seasons, solar and lunar cycles and zodiacal changes in a corresponding pattern. Thus the outer and the inner life reflect each other. The tattwic tides are the working out of the periodic or cyclic law in manifestation. All manifestation is a vibration between poles as we have seen in Chapter One. The actual rhythms, the detailed courses of the flow of energies, and the different levels at which they flow are the tattwic tides. It is a fascinating thought that with a knowledge of the forces which are at work in both the universal and human systems and the directions in which they flow one is actually able to calculate the course of future events.

Ritual

It therefore follows from this that any particular activity which has to be undertaken will be more economically and therefore more effectively performed if it fits in with the prevailing energy flow – or tattwic tides – at that time and place. This is to say that there is an optimum time and place for every activity.

The art of ritual is really the magic of making use of energy to achieve a specific goal. It should be performed in accordance with the prevailing energy tides in order to achieve the most effective results. So that in the widest sense the whole of life can be lived as a ritual in which one is continually making the best of the forces which are dominant to secure the most creative results. Actions are always more effective if performed when the appropriate tattwa relative to that action is manifesting strongly. The direction in which one faces or sleeps, the colours one wears or uses at different times, and in fact every activity in life, is subject to the flow of the tattwas. This is a vast subject which we can only touch on and which it would be out of place to go into more deeply in this work.

The Sign of the Cross

One of the most widely used rituals in the Christian world is the sign of the cross. If one makes the sign of the cross and at the same time has in mind some associations with the crucifixion, one will promote some religious feeling which may be very beneficial. But if one realizes the significance of the ritual in relation to the four pole nature of man and performs it with this knowledge in mind, it becomes a powerful ritual. As the hand moves up and down on the vertical axis and then to the two poles of the horizontal axis the effect is to balance the forces in the system. The ritual should end with a junction of the two hands in the centre and this has the effect of maintaining the equilibrium. We shall see in later chapters the practical significance of balancing the forces in relation to the expansion of consciousness. It is also not generally known that the ritualistic effect of the sign of the cross may be greatly enhanced by combining it with a certain control of the breath.

One of the great conclusions that is to be drawn from this knowledge of the tattwic tides is that in the whole scheme of life every part has its proper function. One should avoid the danger of regarding any centre or level in oneself as being bad. No energy is ever bad in the *absolute* sense, but only it may be used at the wrong time or place. In other words, it may be *relatively* bad, in that it is unbalanced or maladjusted in relation to the whole. We have compared the seven levels of vibration to the musical scale. No note is bad in itself, but if played out of time and place it becomes discordant.

Timing is vital, and the right note must be in the right place. We have to learn to play with all the notes in order to have whole music.

Organs of Action and Sensing

If the four poles of the human system are a fixed magnet and the chakras are the rotors, then the overall pattern is one of seven force fields caused by the quadripolar action at each chakra. As the polarities are reversed, the direction of rotation of the force fields is also reversed. The experience which we have at any of these levels will depend upon whether the energy is incoming or outgoing through that particular chakra. The outgoing energy through a chakra provides us with the organ of activity. That is to say that when the energy is outgoing we have the experience of action at that level; when the energy is incoming we have the experience of sensing at that level.

At each of the five lower chakras, therefore, we have an experience of sense which gives us our five senses. We also have five organs of action which are the same energies in their outgoing aspect.

CROWN	–	Cardinal
BROW	–	Mutable
THROAT	–	Fixed
HEART	–	Air
SOLAR	–	Fire
SACRAL	–	Water
ROOT	–	Earth

At first sight it is not very easy to understand the relationship between these organs of action and sensing. But here let us echo our introductory remarks which point out the limitations of attempted intellectual understanding alone. Through practice and self observation one may come to realize the validity of these abstruse-seeming principles in one's own experience. More comment will be made on the qualities associated with each chakra in the following chapters.

The Middle Pillar

There is another factor of enormous significance in the human system. This is the third force which is known as the *sushumna* in Hindu terminology. The positive and negative currents are termed Pingala or Ida respectively. All manifestation gives rise to a polarity as we have seen in earlier chapters. It is when the positive and negative forces of this polarity are balanced that manifestation ceases. This third force is called the middle pillar in Qabalistic terminology. It is the channel in the centre of the spine through which the energies flow only when the other two forces are balanced. Later we shall examine the practical application of this principle more fully.

Rates of Vibration

The Indian tradition sometimes describes the chakras as lotuses and allocates a certain number of petals to each one. This notion is often confusing to the student until he realizes that this is merely another way of describing the rate of vibration or frequency of the energy at that chakra. The number of petals in each lotus is the same as the number of spokes which each wheel of force has. To illustrate this principle experiments could be made with revolving discs: these would appear to have a varying number of spokes according to the speed at which they revolve.

Similarly the colours which the chakras would throw off also depend upon the speed of their revolution. Colours are light vibrating at different frequencies. Looking at a colour will tend to produce in the viewer a corresponding vibration to that colour. By careful self-observation one may notice the level at which this vibration is seated in oneself. Each chakra has a colour relative to it and will be affected by that colour. What has been said above concerning light also applies equally to the field of sound. Each chakra has a sound relative to it and will be affected by that sound.

Starting at the root chakra and working up to the crown these vibrations are given by the Indian tradition as: 4, 6, 10, 12, 16, 96, 960.

Right- and Left-Sidedness

A subject of interest which opens out from the study of these positive and negative currents is the incidence of right- and left-sidedness in people. Most people have one hand, foot or eye stronger than the other. The reason for this, in effect, is that they have either the positive outgoing or negative receptive side of their nature more highly developed at that level. It may be that in the very highly evolved person these positive and negative forces are equally balanced. It is recounted, for example, of the great adept St Germain, that he could write equally well and at the same time, with both hands.

Attraction and Repulsion

The well-known laws of attraction and repulsion in electricity and magnetism are that like repels like and opposites attract each other. These laws apply to the positive and negative currents in the human system. Sensing and acting are negative and positive. Therefore action in one person is always attracted to receptivity or sensing in another. We see this in the male-female relationship where the active outgoing male nature is paired with the receptive passive female nature.

Through the balancing or mating of two opposite poles a third quality is always born. Each new element or tattwa is formed from the interaction of the positive and negative phases of the preceding one. One may compare this process to that of stirring two ingredients together to produce a third one from their combination. Any new manifestation must always come from the interaction of a positive and negative force, as for example the incarnation of a soul through the union of male and female.

In this connection some light is thrown on the sex of children born; the relative dominance of the positive and negative factors in both mother and father at the time of conception will determine whether the incarnating soul comes in a male or female body.

CHAPTER FOUR

THE QUALITIES OF THE FIVE LOWER CHAKRAS

We shall now try to define the qualities which are associated with each of the five lower chakras, dealing with each in turn. This is to say the actual experience which we have when the energy in our system is focused at that particular chakra.

The Root Centre

The root centre is seated at the base of the spine. At this level the energies manifesting in the human system have reached their slowest rate of vibration. If we think of the energy vibration in terms of sound this would represent the deepest note as produced, for example, by the tuba or double bassoon. In fact music of these coarser vibrations such as military band music or certain kinds of jazz does produce a noticeable effect at the lowest centre and tends to produce the urge to move the feet as in marching, stamping or strutting.

As we explained earlier, the vibration of energy in the human system through a chakra produces an experience which in Hindu terminology is called a tattwa and in Western terms an element. The element of the root chakra is the quality of solidity – in other words the earth element.

The earth element gives us the quality of cohesive resistance and weight of solidness. At this level one has the experience of security and satisfaction in one's existing state and of being comfortable as one is, therefore there is no urge to move or change to another state. The earth element vibration gives one the experience of having one's feet firmly on the ground. It is a very real fact that at times when we feel insecure and nervous the vital currents are not earthed through our lowest centre.

This chakra naturally governs all that is solid in the body such as the bones, teeth and nails. The sense of smell is associated with this level. All creatures that are very close to the earth have a strong sense of smell. We also see this in people; those who are very acute in material matters very often have prominent noses.

The Sacral Centre

The sacral centre is at the level of the sacrum on the spine. At this level we have the experience of fluidity in ourselves. This is called the element of water.

The idea of energy experienced as the principle of fluidity may seem a little mystifying at first sight to the student. We have to adjust to the idea of energy in ourselves at these different levels being experienced as different kinds of consciousness or elements.

For some, the idea of ripeness or smoothness may be a more understandable way of defining the watery quality of this chakra. For example, a fruit's ripeness will require the watery element to be strongly present in it. The same thing applies to people. For man and woman to be ripe from the sexual point of view, the fluid element must be strongly present in their system. The sacral centre is thus connected with the fluid functions of the system such as the urine and the semen.

An insufficiency of the fluid element will lead naturally to aridity. This can cause hardening or drying out diseases such as arthritis. In the latter case the cartilaginous tissue which acts as a natural lubricant between the bones at the joints dries up and painful friction takes place. Ripeness and smoothness give the experience of flow, which is the fluidity of the watery tattwa.

The sense of taste is associated with this level. The English idiom speaks of the mouth watering, and it is the watery element which produces the saliva which makes this possible. The sense of taste is therefore only possible because of the element of water.

The Solar Centre

The solar centre is located on the spine at the level of the solar plexus. At this level we experience the quality of expansiveness, warmth, and joviality in ourselves. This chakra therefore is the seat of the element of fire in our nature.

Fire and water seem to have in a sense opposing qualities. The smooth flow of the watery quality is downward in its direction and is therefore contractive in relation to the essentially upward expansiveness of the fiery quality.

The sense of sight is derived from the activity of this chakra. We can recognize how this comes about when we consider that sight is dependent upon light. But light is a quality of the fire element and is derived from it. Therefore the sense of seeing is only possible because of the fire element.

The strength of the fire element in ourselves at any one time will therefore govern the brightness of what we see. We can recognize the validity of this if we consider how when we are in a certain mood everything we see seems bright and strongly coloured and life seems vivid and warm. At other times we observe the world and we seem to see it as drab, colourless and lifeless. The difference between these two moods is only the relative strength of the solar chakra energy at that time.

The assimilation of food through combustion is governed by the activity of this chakra. The person who has strong vibrations at the level of the solar chakra will absorb great benefit from food he eats. The kind of person who never seems to absorb enough energy from food however much he may eat is deficient in the fire element in his system.

The Heart Centre
The heart centre is located on the spine at approximately the level of the breastbone. At the heart level we experience the qualities of airiness, mobility, gentleness and lightness. These qualities comprise the element of air. They are expressed as 'movement towards' and therefore as relationship or sympathy.

The sense of touch is derived from the element of air. Touch is basically the experience of relationship. We speak of being 'in touch' or 'out of touch'. This is really to say that we have more or less of the heart quality manifesting at that time. It is the air element which gives the relationship experience.

A surplus of any quality becomes a defect. This principle applies to all the chakras. At the heart level too much relationship will become oversympathy and therefore anxiety. An illustration of this point is the state that was described in Victorian days as 'having the vapours'. A surplus of the air or vaporous element in the system produced giddiness or dizziness. The remedy used was smelling salts, because smell is the sense connected with the root chakra or earth element. The energies were therefore brought down to earth and the balance in the system restored.

The Throat Centre
The throat centre is seated on the spine at the level of the throat. At this level we experience the quality of space alone. This is the characteristic of the element of ether.

We have seen that the four lower elements all have qualities which are basically activities within space: ether is the space itself within which these activities take place.

The ether or quintessence, as it was termed by alchemists, is the mixing bowl, so to speak, within which the four lower elements are formed. It is the latency behind them. It is the basis from which each element arises and to which each returns when its period of activity is ended and another element manifests in its place. The four elements are therefore really modifications of the basic ether which can turn itself into any of them. In modern radio terms the ether is the carrier wave for the four elements.

The sense of sound is derived from the element of ether. If one goes to a place where complete and absolute silence reigns and then listens intently, one will eventually become aware of a certain something which is still there behind the silence: a subtle pervasiveness which has been described as the 'noiseless sound'. When one has experienced this one has learned to recognize the etheric element in oneself; but it is more difficult than recognizing the four lower elements.

Through the ether the four elements are controlled. The throat chakra is a vital bridge between the principle of thought at the brow chakra and these four elements. This confirms the biblical dictum 'In the beginning was the Word'. Sound is the most potent of the five lower vibrations and affects them all.

The voice can take on the quality of any of the four lower elements. The voice may be heavy and unresponsive – the sort of voice one associates with solid officialdom – at the earth level. It may be ripe and sexual at the watery level, or warm and passionate at the solar level. The heart voice is gentle and sympathetic. Naturally there are combinations of these qualities and the student can learn much from studying the voice in both himself and in others.

Transmutation of the Elements

In life there is no end – only change. The sum total of energy in the universe does not diminish or increase but continuously transforms itself from one state or level of vibration to another as the flow of life manifests.

As one element comes into manifestation another one withdraws. We can observe this process going on both within and outside ourselves. If, for example, water is frozen, both the fluid and the fire element return to the ether and the solid element arises in their place. If the ice is then brought into contact with heat the solid element returns to the ether from which the fire and water have again manifested. This is really to say that these four elements are the ether which is continually changing its vibrations to manifest itself as them.

We observe these changes outside ourselves as variations in the climatic conditions. There are similar changes going on within ourselves all the time. Heat, for example, will act upon our fluidity and transform it to vapour; so as we become hot we perspire and the activity of the sacral centre is reduced. We may verify this by our own observation that after perspiring fully our sexual activity is always greatly diminished.

The elements are continually flowing in our systems as one succeeds another. However, there is in every human system always a predisposition towards one of them. That is to say that one will tend to be more influential than the others. This is due to the time of one's birth, because at that time one of the elements was predominating in the universal system or zodiac. (We deal with this in more detail in a later chapter.) So when that element is manifesting in your own system you are, so to speak, more at home: hence the saying 'to be in one's element'.

Ether, therefore, always intervenes or rather supervenes between any two of the lower elements as they change over, and it is through the throat that the lower chakras are controlled.

Words are an inadequate medium to describe the subtle qualities of the elements. This is why most systems of teaching use symbols as an aid to recognition. For example, the Hindu tradition makes use of the qualities of certain animals for this purpose: the elephant is used as a symbol for the earth element, embodying as it does the qualities of heaviness and solidity. In many systems diagrammatic symbols are also used which are pictorial representations of the forces which have to be recognized.

Students may find it easier at first to think of the elements simply as moods in themselves. With sustained self-observation one eventually learns to recognize these levels of experience within oneself. Hippocrates, sometimes called the Father of Medicine, based his teaching on the four moods, humours or temperaments. His terminology for the temperaments of phlegmatic, choleric, sanguine and melancholic seem to be naturally related to the earth, water, fire and air tattwas of the four lower chakras.

All disease is due to the forces on the spine becoming out of balance. When the system is out of balance it is no longer whole. The word 'whole' is the same basically as the words 'heal' and 'holy'.

As the life force descends gradually into its lowest vibration at each step it involves itself more deeply into gross matter and each element is formed from the interaction of the positive and negative phases of the previous one. As each new element is formed a new sense manifests. At the etheric level only one sense exists, but at the earth level there are five senses. At the etheric level we can only hear; air, however, can be heard and felt; fire can be heard, felt and seen; water can be heard, felt, seen and tasted; and finally earth can be cognized by all five senses.

To conclude this chapter let us summarize the main points:

Element	Sense	Symbol
Earth	smell	□
Is content to remain where it is and does not want to move or change to any other state.		
Water	taste	☽
Wants to flow downwards and therefore to contract.		
Fire	sight	△
Wants to expand itself and therefore to consume.		

Air   touch

Wants to move to a different
place from where it is and
therefore to relate with
something else.

Ether   sound

Is the space within which
these four elements operate.

CHAPTER FIVE

THE BROW CENTRE

The brow centre is located at the point on the forehead approximately between the eyebrows. The function of the brow chakra is aptly described by its Sanskrit name *Ajna*, meaning command. It is from this level, when we reach it, that we can control or command the whole personality or lower self. This is the seat of mind and at this level we experience mentation; that is to say a flow of mental images and abstract ideas continually coming and going in the mind.

The Power of Thought

Thought is so potent that it materializes itself through the ether. So that what we think, we become. Everything which exists at the material level and which is perceptible to the senses has previously been formed as a mental image in the mind of its creator. Just as the ether is the subtle pervasive substratum of the four lower elements, so thought is the even subtler and more potent principle above the ether. To create anything it is only necessary to think it into existence. However this statement covers an enormous field of practical application and endeavour. It is very hard to bring thought under such control that it forms only those images which we want it to and no others.

The Control of Thought

The control of anything implies not only being able to use it when required but also the ability to cease using it when no longer required. If we cannot stop some process when we want to, then it really controls us, and it is not we who control it. Control of any instrument implies a certain objectivity towards it and therefore a certain independence from it. Consider the analogy of a pot of paint. If one wishes to control this and use it to colour a room one must take care not to become too involved in it. If the paint gets on one's hands then one does not perfectly control the paint. In short, one must be able to keep it at a proper distance or rather keep oneself at a proper distance from it in order to control it.

Control of thought therefore means that we only have in our minds exactly what we wish to have in the shape of ideas and images. It means that when we do not need to use the mind then we can stop thinking at will. Most people still have a long way to go before they can reach this stage and have in their minds only what they want to.

Symbols

The creative power of thought may be harnessed and put to work and one of the most practical ways of doing this is through the use of symbols. A symbol is a key through which we may mentally contact a particular quality which we desire to use. It is an instrument through which we focus mentally on some quality or property which we require to work with. If for example one is feeling nervous and unstable, this will be due to a lack of the earth element in one's system. To counteract this situation and re-establish the balance of the forces one may wish to manifest the earth element in oneself. For those who are used to focusing the mind directly at the different levels this may be almost an automatic process. This process however may be greatly facilitated by the use of a symbol which represents to the user the quality of earthiness. He might use, for example, the mental picture of an elephant. By concentrating on this image he will eventually get beyond and behind the form and find that his mind is gradually assuming the quality symbolized by that form. The mind is, in fact, changing its rate of vibration and entering into the slower earth or root chakra frequency.

There will be an appropriate symbol for every quality or tattwa. However, one should be cautious of accepting any symbol as an absolute, because a symbol that represents a certain quality for one person may very well represent quite another quality to another person by its mental associations. Therefore, perhaps the ideal is to create one's own symbols. Having created the symbol be sure that it is not mentally adulterated by other associations. Its effectiveness will depend upon its purity; that is to say upon its association in the mind of the user with one quality alone.

A mental symbol can be embodied in a material

form such as a statue or medallion, in which case it will become a talisman. Whereas a mental symbol will usually be individual and private to its user, a talisman may be effective independently of its creator. A talisman having been impressed with a certain mental power may be used as an instrument by others.

Telementation

By tuning in to the right mental frequency and wavelength we can communicate directly at the mental level with others no matter what distance apart. We are continually influencing others through our thought and are being influenced by them. Some of us may have had the experience of being with a person who is radiating strong positive and creative thoughts. Although no communication takes place at any other level we immediately begin to feel stimulated. Similarly with people of negative thinking patterns we feel lowered in an apparently mysterious way. Those who are unaware of what is taking place on the subtle levels of thought find these influences inexplicable and disturbing. However, when one understands the potency of the power of thought these effects are seen to be perfectly natural.

The greatest good and harm in the world is brought about by powerful thought currents operating and influencing humanity.

Time

It is activity at the mental level which gives us that experience which we call time. We have seen that in the mind there is a continuous flow of subtle elusive mental pictures as the mind enters into its modifications and transformations. Time is the sequence of these mental pictures. In other words the relationship between two mental pictures is the experience of time passing.

One may helpfully compare this to the moving pictures of a film thrown on to a screen. If firstly a picture of a rosebud is shown and then another picture of the bud opening and finally one of a rose in full bloom, one experiences a sequence of time elapsing. This is a close analogy because the mind is projecting images in the same way and as it does so we make a link or relationship between the pictures either forwards or backwards which we call future or past respectively.

The impression of time either forward into the future or backward into the past is therefore the experience of comparison at the mental level, as two related mental images or impressions are compared together. The relationship between them is the experience of time. The vital point is that when the modifications of the mind are stilled through the concentration and meditation process there is no experience of time at all. Since images do not then arise in the mind there can be no relationship between them and therefore no time. When one is in such a state of consciousness one is aware only of an Eternal Now. As soon as the mind again begins to vibrate and produce impressions and images we establish relationships between them and once again we experience time. In terms of the illustration of the wheel used in Chapter One we have moved inwards from the rim where we experienced separateness and therefore relationship and time to the hub where there is only unity and Now.

Time, therefore, is something that we ourselves create as we produce our own mental images. These images are transient and so past and future are illusory when seen from the standpoint of the spiritual principle. This supervenes only when the mind is still.

We deal with spirit in our next chapter, but let us make a note here that one may use the mind to think about (that is to form a mental idea or concept of) spirit. Many people mistake this process of thinking about spirit for the actual realization of spirit in themselves. But spirit is above the mind altogether. Therefore, the mind deceives us with regard to spirit because the more we think about it the less we realize it.

CHAPTER SIX

THE CROWN CENTRE

The crown centre is located at the top of the head corresponding to the position of the pineal gland. It is the seat of the highest frequency of energy vibration in ourselves.

This vibration is often depicted by artists as a halo surrounding the head of highly evolved or holy people. Statues or pictures of the Buddha usually show the crown chakra at the top of the head. The tonsure practised by monks had its origin in the functioning of this centre. Christian tradition refers symbolically to the twenty-four elders who for ever cast their crowns before the throne of GOD. This also refers to the outpouring of spiritual energy through the crown centre.

The Mystical Marriage

At the mental level there is the experience of objective thought impressions or images arising in the mind. At the spiritual level, there is only the pure subjective experience of *I am* without an objective side. In terms of the Trinity or three gunas, one has discarded or withdrawn from the second and third principles and centred oneself entirely in the first principle. When this has been done one has achieved yoga or union. The lower self has been united with the higher by transmuting the energies from the lower centres to the highest. This is the Mystical or Alchemical Marriage. In Hindu terms it is the Union of the Purusha and the Prakriti.

It is this experience which is referred to in so many of the mystical statements such as '*I am* the Way and the Light'; 'Be still and know that *I am* God'; '*I am* all things to all men'. At the spiritual level there is only the experience of *I am*, but because one has identified oneself with the spiritual or universal principle within oneself, one can speak from the universal level. One can say *I am* and know that the *I* is the whole of life because one has universalized one's consciousness.

'Lo *I* make all things new' also expresses the sense of newness, sometimes referred to as a sense of wonder, experienced at the spiritual level. It is consciousness at the crown chakra which is this experience of the indescribable bliss of union with one's own source – the divine reality within one's own consciousness. It is the mystical experience of all religions. This state has been beautifully described as one of 'isolated unity' and it is truly the experience of aloneness, But, paradoxically this aloneness is All-one-ness which is of course really the origin of the word. At this level one realizes unity with all life; in terms of the symbol of the wheel used in Chapter One, one is at the centre of life and separateness based on objective experience has disappeared. So in order to become one with all life at the spiritual level, it is another paradox that one must move away from it at the outer or personality level.

Many people do not have the courage to renounce attachment at the personal level because they feel that they are separating themselves from life. Only when this renunciation is made does one realize that the only thing one has given up, in fact, is the illusory limitation of the lower self. In doing so one emerges into a higher realm where one is closer to all beings in a unity of a deeper and more real nature. In order to find one's true self one must give up one's lower or illusory self. This finding of the true self corresponds to the transmutation of the energies from the lower chakras to the crown.

Time, which we have seen is the experience of relating mental images to each other as the mind produces thought forms, does not exist at the spiritual level where all is *now* and yet at the time ever new.

Reality and Illusion

In terms of Vedanta the spiritual experience is Advaita or non-duality, because the objective polarity of life ceases so long as one is centred in the subjective Self. Can one remain eternally in this high state? Here we come to one of the subtlest metaphysical questions that can ever be debated. Seen from the standpoint of the time world there is a continuous vibration or rhythm between the poles of spirit and matter and therefore we cannot stay in spirit any more than we can stay asleep all the time. We must always experience the rhythm of sleeping and waking, of inbreathing and outbreathing, birth and death, and all the pairs of opposites which go with the objective world of time and form. It is these rhythms which give us the tattwic tides which is the same thing as the cyclic or periodic law in all manifestation.

Anyone who has meditated will know that he cannot remain for ever in meditation, but after he has contacted the higher levels within he will eventually have to bring these down and express them through creative activity in manifestation. When this expression has been completed he will feel the urge to again return into himself. The bliss of union with the divine principle within is perhaps as relative as any other experience in that its significance lies only in relation to the opposite state – objective duality. Water is only delightful to drink to someone who is dry, heat to one who is cold, and cold to one who is hot.

But looked at from the standpoint of the spirit, can one not say that in reality one never leaves it? This seems to be the traditional Vedanta viewpoint: that the objective world is Maya or illusory in that nothing in it lasts but its forms are continuously appearing and dissolving like the waves of the sea. Only the *I am* consciousness is eternal and changeless.

However, can one not say that even an illusion is real to someone at the time he experiences it? In the Indian parable of the rope and the snake a man mistakes a piece of rope for a snake and is afraid. When he realizes that it is a rope his fear disappears. In fact it was an illusion because it never was a snake. But is it really true to say that it never was a snake? To the experiencer of the illusion its snakeness was perhaps as real at the time as the subsequent experience of it being a rope. The problem when solved appears simple, but for someone who has solved it to keep telling those who have not that it is simple may not be very wise. If someone asks you the way to Hyde Park Corner and you reply that when he gets there he won't need to know the way you are refusing to admit that two standpoints can exist.

CHAPTER SEVEN

BREATH AND THE CHAKRAS

The human breath may be defined as the life force ebbing and flowing between the vertical polarity of spirit and matter (crown and root) and the horizontal polarity of the right and left sides in the human system.

The Great Breath

In the widest sense one speaks of the great breath as being the ebb and flow of the life force between the polarities in the universal system. In fact there is a correspondence between the human or microcosmic energy system and the universal or macrocosmic energy system. One is a reflection of the other and this truth is embodied in the ancient hermetic saying 'as above so below'.

The universal or great breath includes the movement of the planets and heavenly bodies in their periodic cycles, and the signs of the zodiac and the seasons. The human breath similarly has its cycles and seasonal flows. The activities of the chakras correspond to planetary cycles as the planets work through them.

The human breath is not, however, attuned to

the great breath in the lives of most people. This alignment or attunement of the human breath with the great breath is a goal which we have to achieve and represents the complete identification of the personal self with the universal self.

The Rhythm of Breath

The keynote of the breath is flow, and the rhythm of breath in the human system is one of rising and falling of the energies. The fact seems to be seldom fully realized that with the in-breath the energy is drawn upwards to the higher chakras, whilst with the out-breath the energies flow downwards into the world of the senses. Thus, in the literal sense, in-breath is aspiration which takes us upwards into the realm of spirit and out-breath takes us downwards into matter.

Therefore it follows that when we wish to make an effort which involves bringing energy into manifestation on the downward impulse, we should always initially take a deep in-breath. When the lungs are full, the effort itself should then be made on the out-breath. When the lungs are full, the effort itself should then be made on the out-breath. As described in Chapter Three, the breath also moves between the right and left sides of the human System. Thus by this up-and-down and side-to-side movement is built up the spiral pattern of the Caduceus or Staff of Hermes so well known in esoteric symbolism. When electricity is generated the process can be diagrammatically represented on paper as a sine wave thus:

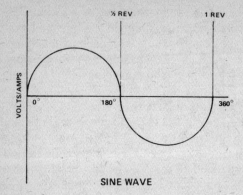

SINE WAVE

By a phase shift of 180° when the impulse reaches
its end it returns. Therefore in electrical terms the
Caduceus is really just two sine waves going out
and returning, called a standing wave.

This side-to-side flow of the breath is reflected in
the manner in which the breath varies between the
right and left nostril. It predominates through one
or the other at certain times. This has already been
touched on in an earlier chapter (see Alternating
Currents, page 30).

By causing the flow of energy to predominate on
the right or left side of our system we can produce
changes in that system. When we are in tune with
the macrocosm these alternations of the breath
occur naturally and at the appropriate times. When
the breath predominates through the right nostril
we have the experience of action. When it
predominates through the left nostril we have the
experience of sensing. This process corresponds to

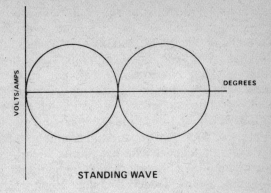

the Pillars of Severity and Mercy in the Qabalistic Tree of Life. When the breath flows equally through both nostrils it has a special significance which we will deal with in the next chapter.

The relative lengths of the in- and out-breaths and the intermediate periods of retention – both in and out – are also of great importance. It is possible to gradually lengthen the period of retention of the breath and this has a spiritualizing effect on one's consciousness. Conversely lengthening the period during which the breath is held out produces the opposite effect. One notices this principle in sighing. An upward sigh reflects an aspirational mood as, for example, when one experiences a sense of wonder at some breathtakingly beautiful scene. A downward sigh reflects a feeling of lethargy as in yawning when one's energies are flowing downwards.

It is sometimes felt that the ideal is to balance the

upward and downward impulses of the life force by an equal rhythm of the in- and out-breath. However, as we have seen, life is a continually changing flow requiring different qualities to manifest at different times. Therefore it seems more logical that we should be able to vary both the upward and downward as well as the left and right rhythms of breath to suit the needs of each moment.

Very few people make the fullest possible use of their potential capacity for breathing. Breath is life and the amount of breath which we can take in is vitally important. Generally, slow breathing will also be deeper breathing, and fast breathing tends to be shallow. Many yogis measure the length of life not by the number of years lived, but by the number of breaths taken. Also there are still many people who have the extremely unhealthy habit of breathing through their mouths.

Regeneration

By emphasizing the in- or upward breath one is spiritualizing or regenerating oneself. *Degeneration* is emphasizing the down-going breath. And *generation* is an appropriate rhythm between the two.

This principle has its interesting counterpart in the field of economics where the process of regeneration corresponds to the activity of investment. By investment one forgoes immediate spending in order to create still greater income later on. It is the principle of saving, or waiting. By regeneration one is reinvesting one's energies in order to promote greater soul growth. Degeneration is too much spending Generation is a balance of spending and saving.

Breath Mantrams

Mantrams used in conjunction with the breath can be helpful to the student. This is a large subject which cannot be fully dealt with here, but an example of this is the *Su Haam* mantram used by yogis. The *Su* sound is uttered on the in-breath and represents the delicate sound of the finer vibrations as the life force moves upwards to the higher chakras. The *Haa* sound, uttered on the out-breath, represents the coarser sound of the lower vibrations as the life force descends. The *m* at the end of *Haam* is produced by closing the mouth, and this *m* has the effect of making the sound objective.

The breath seems to take on the form of the particular tattwa (shown on page 47) which is predominating in the system at any one time. It is said that this can be seen by projecting the breath on to a mirror. Recently some scientific research has been done in photographing etheric forms which seems to bear this out.

Control of the Breath

Patient observation of one's own breathstream eventually leads to the ability to control the vital forces and focus them at will at the different levels. Gradually one learns to recognize the changes in vibration which occur as the breath or life force passes through the different levels. In this way one learns to control the elements or tattwas.

So long as the breath is ebbing and flowing we

are living in the world of polarities – the world of form. The ultimate step in control is when the breath is suspended altogether and one leaves the world of form and withdraws into the spiritual realm, the universal consciousness. Only the adept can withdraw completely in this way.

Withdrawal, however, is very much a matter of degree. It is through the same gateway that one passes in sleep, death, or in deep meditation, but only the degree of withdrawal is different.

Sleep
The depth of sleep varies greatly with different people. Some hardly leave the body or sense consciousness during sleep. Others leave the sense consciousness but remain active at the mental level experiencing dream states. Some are able to withdraw from the body and mind and remain at a still higher level from which they return truly refreshed when they awake.

Death
The same principle applies to death where the level to which the soul may reach will depend on its evolutionary progress. Some souls remain practically earthbound even after discarding the physical body. Often they are already seeking to reincarnate or sometimes to experience the sense world again through an incarnate soul whom they may try to influence or possess. Others will pass peacefully to higher states. They may first renew relationships with other discarnate souls and eventually pass to still higher 'summerlands' to

renew themselves completely until the impulse to express themselves in form leads them once more to incarnate.

Deep Meditation

In deep meditation one is consciously doing, or attempting to do, what most people do more or less involuntarily in sleep and death. One is withdrawing to that level within, where one renews oneself at the eternal fountain of life – one's own spiritual source.

This process too is a matter of degree according to proficiency. The adept who has learned to control his breath or life force at all levels is able to suspend it and withdraw from his body, but without abandoning it. He is also able to return to it again when he needs to. By consciously dying at the necessary times in order to renew himself he avoids the need to die involuntarily in the common way.

Such an adept might require a long life span extending perhaps over several centuries in order to complete some important work for the evolution of humanity. Therefore he would retain the same body during that period by renewing himself in this way. This might be especially necessary in view of the difficulty for such a highly evolved soul in finding the suitable circumstances into which he could reincarnate through birth. Such an adept would at the end of a life cycle dematerialize his body when his work at that level was completed.

Life Cycles

The length of one's life is really proportionate to the

soul or higher self's motive for living. When the soul
has exhausted its purpose it withdraws having used
up its downward impulse. A high sense of purpose
is derived from spirit, and so when its purpose is
exhausted it must renew itself in spirit by
withdrawal. All life manifests in cycles. Each in –
and out – breath, each day and night of waking and
sleeping, each life and death in a body, these are all
the same principle, but operating at a larger or
smaller scale. They are all the periodic or cyclic law
operating as life vibrates between its poles.

CHAPTER EIGHT

PRACTICE

The science of the chakras is very much the science of *breath* and *posture*. In order to fully appreciate their enormous significance these two terms have to be understood in their widest sense. *Posture* is to be understood as one's total attitude to life at all levels. Therefore one can speak not only of physical but also of mental and spiritual posture. *Breath* is to be understood as the movement of the life force throughout the entire system; as the flow of energy between its poles of spirit and matter.

Bearing these principles in mind and with the knowledge of man's occult anatomy outlined in the first part of this book, the purpose behind the practices of yoga becomes very much clearer.

Preliminaries

Any serious programme or system of self-training has to begin with attention to the basic rules of health at the simplest levels. These may be compared to the foundations of a house. One may neglect the foundations at first with apparent impunity. But later on when more weight is added to the structure the building will not stand up. The same principle applies to self-training. Building on an insecure foundation means eventually having to go back on one's work to remedy the defects. For as one goes higher in self-training one contacts greater energies and brings these into activity in one's system. If the system is not strong enough it will not be able to contain them. This may be compared to pouring very hot water into a container which has flaws in it and therefore breaks up.

These basic rules are to be found in all the classical systems. Harmlessness to all life, truthfulness, cleanliness, right diet, freedom from excesses in any field – all these qualities are the equivalent of the foundations of our building. A foundation is a basic strength upon which to build and these virtues are in fact strengths of character upon which we can build our higher development.

HATHA YOGA

The next step is the work of balancing the lower energies in the system. Many people do not understand why the Hatha yoga postures and exercises are really necessary in self-development. They try to take a short-cut by omitting the whole of this initial but vital part of the process.

Let us take a simple illustration which makes this point quite clear. If one attempts to balance a pencil upright on its end at first it is necessary to keep steadying it with the hand to prevent it falling over. When it is balanced, however, one can remove one's hand and it will remain upright. Now consider the body as the pencil. The aim of Hatha yoga is to bring the body to such a state of health and perfection that its forces are balanced. Only then can one withdraw one's attention from it and concentrate one's attention at higher levels. In fact so long as the body is not in perfect equilibrium the attention of the mind will be continually absorbed in it in just the same way as the hand's attention was continually absorbed in steadying the pencil until it was balanced.

We have all at some time had the experience of being unable to sleep due to pain in some part of our body. At such times the consciousness is continually absorbed in, and therefore attached, to this pain, so that it is unable to leave the body. When the pain ceases, however, the consciousness can leave it and pass upwards into the sleep state. The whole aim of Hatha yoga is to be found in this analogy. It is to bring the body into such a state of equilibrium that the consciousness can be withdrawn from it and pass upwards to higher states.

In terms of the chakras, Hatha yoga prepares the energies at the lower levels to be raised to the higher ones. When the energies have been so raised the preliminaries are no longer so necessary.

This point is made clear in the classical yoga textbook the *Hatha Yoga Pradipika* which says that the various asanas, kumbakhas and mudras should be practised 'so long as Raja Yoga has not been attained'.

However, it is also possible to practise Hatha yoga without having much understanding of its real purpose. A great deal of yoga practised both in the West and East falls into this category and has become merely a fashionable new kind of gymnastics. Many people, not realizing that this is a means to a higher goal, make it an end in itself so that it becomes a glamorous kind of acrobatics or contortionism. Of course even with this limited motive the practitioner will still derive benefit to his health but the real purpose will have been missed.

Clearing the Nadis

With a knowledge of man's occult anatomy and a clear idea of the aim of yoga, the purpose of many practices becomes easier to understand. Initially the aim of these practices is to free the posture from any blockages or kinks which may be inhibiting it. Nearly everyone has some blockage at some points in his system: that is to say, there is a resistance at some point to the flow of the energies. In fact all disease is merely a restriction of the flow of the life force in a particular area. In yoga terminology the channels through which the energies flow in the human system are called *nadis*. These nadis have to be cleared of blockages and enlarged. This process is an important part of Hatha yoga. Exercises and postures which involve bending, twisting and stretching the spine fall into this category of generally promoting greater energy flow throughout the system.

Balancing Postures

Another important category of postures is those which promote balance. We have seen that balancing the forces has a vital significance especially when we come to the question of the third force or kundalini. Postures and exercises which train one in the art of balancing are important in learning to control the positive and negative forces in the system and bringing them into equilibrium.

The Lotus Posture

The lotus posture and its variations has a combination of effects. First, it provides a stable triangular base on which the spine and upper part of the body can be supported at ease. This is essential for later stages of meditation and concentration. If correctly performed it also has the effect of causing the spinal column to be held erect on the pelvis. Secondly, by crossing the legs and either joining the hands or placing them on the knees, the open energy circuits are closed. Energy which would normally leave the system through the hands and feet is therefore retained. Slight pressure from the heel on the perineum aids the upward flow of energies from root to crown. Thirdly, this posture is essentially a sublimative one. Through its practice the energies in the system are retained, brought under control, and sublimated up the vertical polarity of the spine to the higher centres.

After the preliminaries a further stage can be reached when certain practices which directly affect the chakras may be undertaken. The subtle effects which various postures, mudras and bandhas have on the energies in the system is an extremely complex and difficult subject. Very few of those who practise yoga seem to understand fully these effects. Some portions relating to this subject are kept secret. However by correlating the explanations of man's occult anatomy already given with his own experiences in practice, the student can work these out for himself to a great extent.

We give certain examples which may serve as guidelines in this field: inverted postures for instance cause the energies to flow upwards to the higher chakras. The comparison of an ordinary electrical battery is helpful here. Current flows between the positive and negative poles. When the battery is discharged the method of recharging is to reverse the flow of current through it between its poles. In the human system by standing on one's head one is doing just the same thing; reversing the flow of energy between the polarities on the vertical axis of the spine.

The student will also readily be able to realize for example that the throat and heart are strongly affected by certain postures. In particular the shoulder stand has a remarkable effect on the throat centre provided that the body is held absolutely erect and at right angles to the neck with the chin pressed firmly against the sternum. Bow postures with the breath retained cause energies to flow into these chakras provided the head is fully held back.

As a further example, certain postures are effective in activating the solar chakra. These are principally the ones which draw in the abdomen and exercise control over the energies centred there. After practising these correctly one becomes aware of a greatly increased activity of the gastric fire or fire element in the system. Similarly the sacral and root centres are affected by their appropriate postures.

These postures and exercises should always be practised:

(*a*) With a knowledge of the purpose and effect which they are intended to promote.

(*b*) Slowly and deliberately without hurry or anxiety.

(*c*) With complete one-pointed concentration on what is being done.

Kundalini

The best way to understand the mysterious third force or kundalini is by the illustration of the pendulum. When the pendulum is in motion it swings continuously from side to side vibrating between horizontal or right and left poles. It also has a vertical polarity and as it swings, energy is transmitted downwards from its pivot or source. If its motion ceases the right and left poles become balanced and cease to exist. Then the energy which was being sent downwards must also return to its source and travels upwards along the pendulum which is now stationary in the middle.

In yoga terminology the right and left side energy flows are *Pingala* and *Ida*, and the central channel is *Shushumna*. In Qabalistic terms they are the Pillars of Severity and Mercy and the central channel is the Path of the Arrow. Kundalini, therefore, is the path by which the energy returns to its source when it ceases to manifest in the human system as a vibration between poles. When kundalini returns to its source the pendulum has ceased to swing. All polarity ceases and our consciousness returns to its source through the crown chakra. When the breath

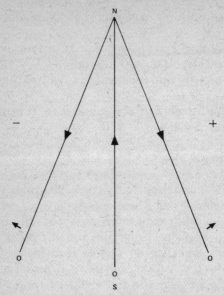

ceases to flow through the right and left sides of the
system either we die or if we have prepared
ourselves and the energy is controlled, we can
transcend death and can pass consciously into the
deep mystical state of *Samadhi*.

There is considerable misunderstanding
concerning the awakening of forces in the human
system which then, it is said, activate the chakras.
On the whole this is putting the cart before the
horse; it is truer to say that when the nadis or
energy channels are purified, and the forces are
balanced, the chakras are ready; then the energies
can flow through them and not vice versa.

In all nature forced growth is never the most

healthy kind of growth, and sudden dramatic awakenings of forces are seldom desirable. Instances of this kind of unbalanced development seem to have received more publicity than they merit and are often assumed to be the rule rather than the exception. There are, however, certain people in whose lives the awakening of forces or faculties is likely to be very sudden and perhaps unexpected. This is due to karmic forces building up gradually against some strong obstacle or deep-rooted hindrance to that person's development. In such a case the obstacle will go on resisting until the forces building up finally overcome it and as a result a sudden change in the pattern of life and its energy flow comes about.

At a later stage the highly evolved soul learns to control the powerful awakened energies which flow through his system. He will be able to direct them upwards or downwards, or focus them at whatever level he requires. For some people the effect of the sublimation of the awakened kundalini will be one of rejuvenation. One is reminded of Rider Haggard's 'She' who preserved the prime of her body by bathing in the sacred fire in the mountain. It is interesting to speculate how much the author knew of the esoteric aspect of his subject concerning the real sacred fire within.

RAJA YOGA

The Mind
The mind is often compared by yoga teachers to a pond, the surface of which is covered with

innumerable ripples caused by the winds of desire blowing upon the water and ruffling it. Only when these winds cease to blow does the water cease to be agitated. Then it becomes calm and lucid and a totally new experience supervenes because it is possible to look down through it and see the bedrock of the pond beneath. Previously, due to the water's agitation, one could not have seen the bedrock of the pond or known that it existed. In this analogy the water of the pond is of course the mind, and its substratum or bedrock is the higher principle within ourselves which is above the mind – the spiritual consciousness. The winds of desire are the emotions which ruffle the mind.

Desire and Emotions

True concentration of the mind is therefore only possible when we can achieve dispassion and detachment from our emotions. We have seen already that thought descends through the etheric level to manifest through the four elements, which are themselves modifications of the ether. Whenever the mind, therefore, is associated with any of the elements it is in a state of emotion. In terms of the chakras, when the energy of the brow chakra begins to take on the vibrations of any of the five lower chakras its own vibration is lowered and it becomes tinged by emotion. Every emotion is an association of the thought principle with one or more of the elements which then colour or condition it. Pure thought, uncoloured by any of the lower vibrations, is the unconditioned mind.

Unconditioned Thought

The unconditioned mind is free from the organs of sensing or acting associated with the lower chakras and is self-contained in its own vibration. Such pure thought is tremendously potent. Faculties such as thought transference, materialization, and mind reading depend upon the ability to concentrate the mind by freeing it in this way. As we have already seen earlier in this chapter the ability to do this depends initially on proper preliminary training at the Hatha yoga level. Thus Hatha yoga leads on to Raja yoga in a natural sequence of progress.

Transcending Thought

Finally the energy of the brow chakra must be raised to the higher vibratory rate at the crown. This step is only possible and should only be attempted after the mind has been thoroughly disciplined and a high level of mental concentration achieved.

In order to have complete control of any instrument one must be able to take it up, use it efficiently, and lay it down again at will. Only then does it become a true instrument. Only then can one stand back from it and say, 'This is my instrument, it is not me; I am separate from it and I control it'.

The mind has to be trained to this degree before the final stage can be achieved. The thoughts have to be brought under complete control. Only then can we make the subtle distinction between the thought and the thinker. When we realize that *I the thinker exist independently of my thought* we can lay down the thought and remain conscious at the *I am* level alone. Then we cross the final bridge from *Not Self* to *Self*.

Dangers in Practice

Many students are concerned about the possible dangers involved in the practice of yoga, especially if self-taught. Some comment on this question would seem to be appropriate here. First, one should realize that danger is a relative term. What is dangerous for one person may be completely safe for another. Therefore one cannot logically say that anything is dangerous in itself except in relation to the person doing it. Secondly, everything in life that one does carries some element of risk. If there were no risk at all in that activity then the return or results from it would be negligible in creative importance. The reward is always proportionate to the effort involved, and the effort required will be proportionate to the relative danger.

So the whole of life is a process of learning from experiences which when looked back on afterwards appear as mistakes by comparison with our subsequent knowledge. Therefore one needs to be ready to go forward boldly but not rashly into the future ready to improve on what one did before. To take more risk than one can comfortably handle is foolhardy and not to take any risk is equally foolish.

A Guru

Undoubtedly a competent teacher will help one progress more swiftly, but in the matter of finding such a teacher an important point is often overlooked. It is you yourself who in the end has to decide whether or not a certain person is a competent teacher and so the responsibility must finally come back to yourself.

No one can do your learning for you just as no one else can eat your food for you. There will be no progress without a willingness to assume responsibility. In this connection there is a further even more important point, which is that in accordance with the law of karma or cause and effect, one ultimately receives from life what one puts into it. What one gives out and what one receives are two sides of the same coin. However, a great part of humanity has not yet learned this truth which is naturally linked with the law of reincarnation, since the giving out and receiving back is necessarily evened out over more than one life.

This law applies equally to learning in that one may only receive knowledge to the extent that one gives it out. Therefore in order to learn one must also teach what one knows to others who need it. The latter comment involves an important principle of using one's energy in the most economical and therefore most creative way. To give to someone exactly the most useful knowledge that he needs at the moment he needs it is to do this. Trying to force knowledge on people who are not ready for it is a wasteful and therefore an uncreative use of energy. In this, discrimination is necessary to judge whom you can best help, and in which way, and at what time. The door-to-door apostle trying to force his ideas on all and sundry lacks proper discrimination and makes an uneconomical use of energy.

The old adage that when one is ready the teacher will appear is true because you bring yourself by your own efforts into contact with the sources of knowledge which you merit at that time. But even the best teacher can only teach one to teach oneself.

CHAPTER NINE

THE RIGHT USE OF ENERGY

There is a natural tendency to regard any programme of self-improvement as if it were a journey leading to an ultimate destination. This destination is often thought of as final perfection towards which man is continually growing through a process of evolution. It is seen as union with the divine life from which man has become separated and to which he returns along a path of unfoldment.

But although this concept serves a useful purpose for man at a certain stage of his development it has eventually to be superseded by an even higher one. For it is not that the road leads to a final goal, but rather that the road itself is the goal. We tend to represent the journey in terms of space and time as if life came to a stop when we reached a certain point. But really life itself is infinite – it is not static but a dynamic continuum. So that although one needs at a certain stage to think of a goal as an incentive to growth, the end is really endlessness itself.

The idea of life being endless or eternal is something for which most people are not ready. To let oneself go forward into the eternal flow of life without thought of any end is a stage which needs courage and is also a great challenge. This principle helps us greatly where yoga is concerned because yoga too is its own reward. It does not need an end or goal in terms of time. If one's practice makes one more joyful then this is the criterion of progress. Joy is the expansion of consciousness or the principle of 'moreness'. Suffering is the limitation of consciousness, the principle of 'lessness'.

Energy is in Proportion to Motive

Everything in the universe radiates some form of energy, whether it be mineral, vegetable, animal or human. The amount of its radiation is in proportion to its relationship to the total or universal energy. So where the energy system of man is concerned the amount of energy on which he can draw is in exact proportion to the universality or otherwise of his own consciousness. The more selfish and limited his motives in life, the more he shuts himself off from the wholeness of life, and the less the life force will flow through him. In short, energy is in proportion to motive.

Many of us will have had the experience of undertaking some activity in a spirit of fear, hatred, doubt or with some other selfish motive; this always leaves one feeling utterly exhausted. By contrast, those who act with a selfless, universal motive of service and of giving will know that such work brings no tiredness in its wake but in fact brings joy and renewed energy. To the extent that our motive is for the good of the whole, to just that extent do we have the right to draw on the whole or universal energy. In reality life has no shortage or limitation. Energy is limitless and life itself is abundance. It is we who put limitation into life by our finite motives. The measure of a man's greatness or degree of evolution is his capacity for giving.

Nature, it has been said, abhors a vacuum. As we give out energy new life flows in to fill the space. But when we hold back and restrict our creative activity we experience a lack of vital force because we have not allowed the life to flow through us. One may compare this process to that of a water pump which can only receive through its inlet to exactly the same extent that it gives out through its outlet. As we create and receive back we fulfil this law of energy and 'give that we may receive and give again'. Every selfish or limiting action diminishes the flow of life through us; every universal or expanding action increases it.

These principles are often referred to as the laws of universal supply and those who understand and live by them know no shortage but flow joyfully and abundantly through life as a bird flies undoubtingly through the air. Such people make life an adventure – an unending exploration of life's infinite possibilities. This also means of course the infinite possibilities within oneself.

This principle of flowing continuously forward with life's becomingness is symbolized in several age-old parables. There is for example the story of Lot's wife. In the journey away from the city of evil she was turned into a pillar of salt because she looked back. By looking backward one loses the flow of creativity which is essentially a forward-going force and so crystallization sets in. The same principle is symbolized in the story of Orpheus redeeming his beloved from the underworld. He could only save her if he did not look back but kept moving onwards and forwards. As he lost confidence in the future and therefore lost his faith, he looked back and so failed to redeem his imprisoned love or life force.

The Best Use of Energy

Just as water flows downhill following the line of least resistance, so energy always flows to its most useful field of activity. When one field of activity has fulfilled its purpose the life force flows forward into another field. In this way evolution follows a law, for the energy is always moving into that field of activity where it can manifest most creatively. The sum total of energy in the universe does not increase or diminish but is continuously being transformed or transmuted from one state to another. Cessation of activity in one field always means a renewal of activity in another field.

Dharma

This concept of energy flowing to its next most useful task in the evolutionary pattern is embodied in the idea of dharma. Everyone is climbing an evolutionary ladder; therefore in relation to all his circumstances there will be an optimum action for each person at any one time in his life. The next step on the evolutionary ladder for any one person at any one time is his dharma. This is to say that it is the next action into which his energies can best be channelled in order for them to manifest in the most creative possible way.

Control of Energy Through Yoga

The foregoing principles involving the right use of energy are all embodied in the practice of yoga. The flow of life is in fact the breathstream in the human system. The channels through which it flows are the nadis. The different levels at which it manifests are the tattwas. When our flow of creativity seems to dry up then we have to look to the nadis and chakras for the remedy. The breath and posture will somewhere have become blocked. Through yoga one may release the blockages and once more become creative and full of energy. Through yoga we identify our human energies with the universal energies. Just as life itself is infinite and eternal, so our consciousness can become limitless in all its possibilities through yoga.

CHAPTER TEN

ASTROLOGY AND THE CHAKRAS

The relationship between astrology and yoga seems to be only very slightly appreciated. It merits much greater study than it has hitherto enjoyed. There are many aspects of this relationship that are not clear and in which there is enormous scope for further research.

The Flow of All Things

That there is a continual flow of becoming in all life has been understood by both Eastern and Western philosophers throughout the ages. Greek philosophers used the phrase '*Π* AVTA REI' (*panta rei*) – 'all things flow'; and Hindu sages used the word *Samsara* – 'the world of becoming'. Astrologers study this flow of becoming through the movement of the planets and heavenly bodies in the zodiac and in its signs and houses.

In general, astrologers see man as being subjected to influences from these planets. Very few astrologers seem to take their science further by enquiring *how* these influences can be effective on the human system. One can easily overlook the fact that any influence can only make itself effective on some object *through a corresponding vibration in that object*. Without such an attunement there can be no rapport or influence between them. It is through the vital centres or chakras that the influences of the planets become effective in the human system.

'As Above So Below'

However, it would be a one-sided view of the subject to look only at the influence of the heavenly bodies on Man's system. Could it not be equally true that the opposite also applies? Each affecting the other? For Man's system of energy flows and his network of chakras is an exact correspondence of the universal system. It is a microcosm of the macrocosm. Can one then say that either affects the other exclusively? It is perhaps truer to say that each is a reflection of the other. The outer and the inner, the above and the below, must both co-exist in reality. One cannot have a top without a bottom or an inside without an outside and so one cannot have a microcosm without a macrocosm.

The Chakra Zodiac

Let us now trace the correspondence between the outer or astrological zodiac and what we may call the inner or chakra zodiac. The astrological zodiac is formed through the interaction of the higher triplicity or three primary energies and the lower quaternary or four secondary energies as explained previously. The four lower energies we have already seen are the elements. Astrologers term the three primary energies *cardinal, mutable,* and *fixed*. Each of the four elements is modified by one of the three primary energies and is therefore in one of three possible states of vibration. Thus is produced a twelve-fold division of the universal system. These twelve divisions of energy have each a predominant characteristic described by symbols or signs with which most students are familiar.

In Man's occult anatomy as we have already seen, the three primary energies have their seats at the three higher chakras. The four lower chakras are the seats of the four elements. Similarly in the universal zodiac each element is modified by one of the three primary energies, so that it is in either a

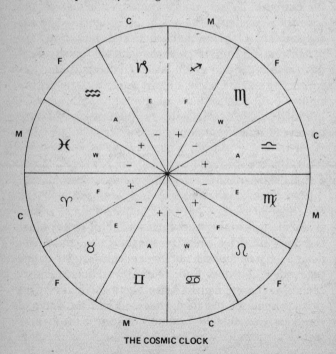

THE COSMIC CLOCK

cardinal, mutable, or fixed state. Therefore, in accordance with this logical sequence, each sign of the zodiac is made up of a relationship between two chakras in Man's system; one from the higher three of the trinity and one from the lower four of the quaternary.

We take for example the sign Taurus. Being of fixed earth we find that its qualities are effective in the human system by a relationship between the throat chakra in the trinity and the root chakra in the quaternary. This would appear to correctly give the extremely fixed characteristic of the sign. If we take the sign Gemini, being mutable air, following the same rules we arrive at a relationship between the brow chakra and the heart chakra. Here again the result appears to correctly produce the extremely mobile and mentally agile quality of this sign.

Many aspects of this fascinating subject, however, require further research. In particular the order in which the three qualities and the elements are taken in the zodiac needs to be studied. Does this accord with the order of their involution along the vertical polarity of man's spinal axis? There may at first sight appear to be conflict in the sequence in which these are taken. The astrological convention by which each sign rules a part of the body running from head to toe needs also to be critically examined. Each of the five lower chakras has its own organs of sense and action. These relate to its positive or negative phase. Can these parts of the body therefore be related equally to the twelve signs?

The Significance of Birth Time

The significance of the time of birth is that it is the point at which we enter the flow of becoming. The flow of manifestation continues, and souls enter it or incarnate into it at various points. The characteristics which are manifesting at that point in time will be the ones which the incarnating soul takes on. It requires these in that life in order to have the experiences necessary for its evolution. We have seen that each experience follows logically from the previous one as the energy flows to its next most useful expression. Therefore from a knowledge of astrology it is possible to predict the future events in any incarnation; even further, the time of future incarnations and under what signs they will be can be predicted.

But when one refers to a knowledge of astrology one means not only a knowledge of the facts upon which it rests, but also the ability to interpret the significance of the data. To record and set down data is the first step, to correctly interpret its meaning and significance is a much greater ability.

The Flow of the Tattwas and the Zodiac

The zodiacal changes correspond to the flow of the tattwas in the human system. Therefore one can read the zodiac and from it see what changes will occur in one's life, or one can determine from the flow of tattwas in one's own system what changes will occur in one's own astrological chart. Yoga at its highest level identifies with astrology. The relationship between the universal breath and pilman breath can be traced numerically. The universal Zodiac revolves in 25550 years, giving each sign or age a span of approximately 2145 years. This fact is at present much before the public eye as we leave the Piscean Age and approach the new Aquarian Age. The normal human breath rate of about 18 per minute also gives 25550 breaths in a full day. Furthermore, 25550 days gives a life span of 70 years (the average three score and ten for the Piscean age). Thus the rate of breath, length of life span and duration of universal Zodiac are all related in one rhythm.

At first sight it may seem difficult to understand that through the interaction of only seven levels of consciousness an infinite variety of experiences is possible. Let us explain this by a musical analogy. Any experience is relative to the previous one. Let us suppose, for example, that one plays the note G after the note A. The experience one has from listening to that note will be different from what it would be if one previously heard the note C. In short the previous event modifies the subsequent experience. Not only does the previous note determine the experience gained by hearing the subsequent one but their relative durations also influence the experience. One C coming after three Gs is a different experience from one G followed by three Cs. Two or more notes played at the same time further varies the experience.

Where colour is concerned the same principle applies. Looking at red after blue gives one a different experience from looking at red after green. The length of time each colour is looked at and the combination of colours further varies the experience. The principle can be carried further because the experience before the previous one also modifies the subsequent experience; so does the one before that and the one before that, *ad infinitum*.

Applying these colour and sound analogies to the chakras (to which they correspond) we see that from our chakra zodiac an infinite variety of experiences is produced.

Planets and Chakras

The planets are the equivalent in the universal system of the chakras in the human system. In effect they are the universal chakras. Therefore there must be correspondences between the planets and the human chakras. It seems that in relating the planets to the chakras one should observe some logical sequence such as their distance from the earth or relative speeds of movements. A cardinal tenet of astrology is that every hour and every day is under the influence of a planet. The seven days of the week are named after the planets which rule the first hour of each day. The succession begins with the most distant planet Saturn and takes them in their order of distance from the earth, and in the order of speed from slowest to swiftest. This also corresponds to their relative speeds. Starting with Saturn's day (Saturn ruling the first hour): Jupiter rules the second hour; Mars the third; Sun the fourth; Venus the fifth, Mercury the sixth; Moon the seventh. Each planet influences the first hour of its own day and also the eighth, fifteenth and twenty-second hour. Thus when we arrive at the twenty-fourth hour the ruler is Mars, and we start

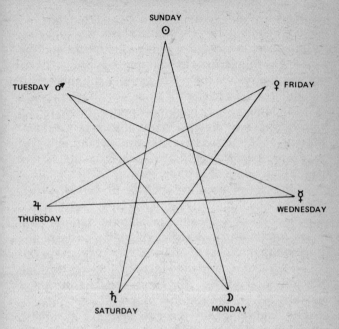

the next day with Sun's day. Then, following the same order of repetition the Moon rules the next day and so on throughout the week. There is one hour of the day for each of the seven planets.

A relationship between planets and chakras could be established on some similar basis. However, it would seem to be an oversimplification to conclude that one planet always corresponds exclusively to one chakra. It seems more correct to say that the relationship is a variable one and also that it differs for the male and female.

Aspects

Relationships between planets in the universal system give us aspects or patterns of influence from which meanings may be interpreted. Similarly, in the human system the relationship of the energies at the different chakras gives us aspects in the chakra zodiac. However, although on paper the system is represented two-dimensionally, it is in fact a three-dimensional system. In understanding the relationships between various parts of the system this fact needs to be kept in mind.

The greatest occultist Helena Blavatsky wrote: 'Its one absolute attribute which is itself eternal ceaseless motion is called in esoteric parlance *The Great Breath* which is the perpetual motion of the universe in the sense of limitless ever-present space.'

The greath breath is the outer life flowing through the universal zodiac. *The human breath* is the inner life flowing through the chakra zodiac.

The knowledge of the rise and fall of breath comprehends all knowledge.

It is the highest of all sciences.